IRON ROSE

IRON ROSE

The Story of
Rose Fitzgerald Kennedy
and Her Dynasty

CINDY ADAMS
and
SUSAN CRIMP

DOVE
BOOKS

ISBN 0-7871-0475-2

Printed in the United States of America

Dove Books
301 North Cañon Drive
Beverly Hills, CA 90210

Distributed by Penguin USA

Text design by Stanley S. Drate/Folio Graphics Co., Inc.

FIRST PRINTING: AUGUST 1995

10 9 8 7 6 5 4 3 2

Acknowledgments

"Writing about the Kennedy family makes me even more aware of the only family I have. . . .

To my Joey . . ."

—CINDY ADAMS

"To Rose Kennedy who lived 104 years to make this story possible. May her strength be an inspiration to us all."

—SUSAN CRIMP

Special Acknowledgements

Tremendous thanks have to go to all the people, who spent endless hours in all weathers helping us cover the Kennedy family. Frank Caponegro, Mario Porporino, Anthony Salerno, Sam Somwaru, Gus Roccaforte, Kim Maitland, Gary McCafferty, Justin Heid, Lisa Katz, Phyllis Zimmerman, Frank Grimes, Julie Harman, Teddy Corriero, Paul and Roberta Adao, Steve Connolly, Angie Coqueren, Ken Katz. For their assistance: Melody Miller, Gail Fee, Lester David, John H. Davis, and Wendy Leigh. Special thanks also go to Linda Bell and the Hard Copy team in Los Angeles for allowing us to chronicle the Kennedy dynasty with grace and elegance. Mary Aarons for all her help in shaping this project. And, finally, thanks to Milton Goldstein our computer man for his devotion in seeing us through.

"In times of tragedy, her faith has been her great strength. She has, by her example, made us all realize the importance of God in our lives. She has often said that she does not believe God gives us a greater cross than we can bear, and she remains an eternal optimist.

"Her strength helped the family survive the great grief over the loss of my brothers and sister, and I called on her example to help my son Teddy when he lost his leg to cancer."

"My sister Rosemary is mentally retarded, and that was a great sorrow to my mother and all of us. But she was brought up in our family and my mother made a great effort to have her included in our activities. If we were going sailing or to a dance, we were encouraged to take her with us for part of the time, and no one spent more time helping her than my mother. Seeing all of her effort made us want to help too."

—Senator Edward Kennedy
Interview with Susan Crimp
Hello Magazine, 1990

I get up every morning and I shake my fist at God and I say, "I will not be defeated."

—Rose Fitzgerald Kennedy
1970's

The Rose Still Grows Beyond the Wall

Near a shady wall a rose once grew
Budded and blossomed in God's free light
Watered and fed by morning dew,
Shedding its sweetness day and night.

As it grew and blossomed fair and tall,
Slowly rising toward loftier height,
It came to a crevice in the wall,
Through which there shone a beam of light.

Onward it crept with added strength,
With never a thought of fear or pride,
It followed the light through the crevice's length,
And unfolded itself on the other side . . .

—Almira L. Frink

Contents

Contents

Part Two

1945–1968:
The Brightest Lights

Part Three

1969–1994:
A Fine Age

Contents

THE KENNEDY FAMILY

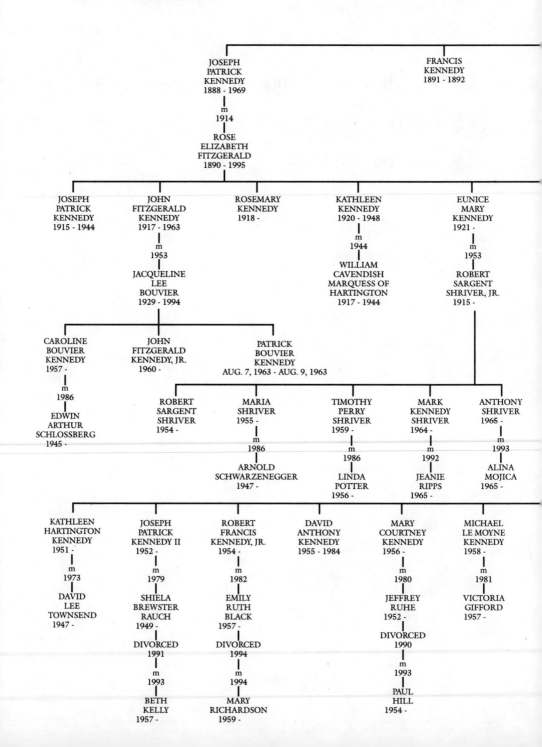

PATRICK
KENNEDY

JOSEPH
PATRICK
KENNEDY
1888 - 1969

FRANCIS
KENNEDY
1891 - 1892

m
1914

ROSE
ELIZABETH
FITZGERALD
1890 - 1995

JOSEPH
PATRICK
KENNEDY
1915 - 1944

JOHN
FITZGERALD
KENNEDY
1917 - 1963

ROSEMARY
KENNEDY
1918 -

KATHLEEN
KENNEDY
1920 - 1948

EUNICE
MARY
KENNEDY
1921 -

m
1953

m
1944

m
1953

JACQUELINE
LEE
BOUVIER
1929 - 1994

WILLIAM
CAVENDISH
MARQUESS OF
HARTINGTON
1917 - 1944

ROBERT
SARGENT
SHRIVER, JR.
1915 -

CAROLINE
BOUVIER
KENNEDY
1957 -

JOHN
FITZGERALD
KENNEDY, JR.
1960 -

PATRICK
BOUVIER
KENNEDY
AUG. 7, 1963 - AUG. 9, 1963

m
1986

EDWIN
ARTHUR
SCHLOSSBERG
1945 -

ROBERT
SARGENT
SHRIVER
1954 -

MARIA
SHRIVER
1955 -

TIMOTHY
PERRY
SHRIVER
1959 -

MARK
KENNEDY
SHRIVER
1964 -

ANTHONY
SHRIVER
1965 -

m
1986

m
1986

m
1992

m
1993

ARNOLD
SCHWARZENEGGER
1947 -

LINDA
POTTER
1956 -

JEANIE
RIPPS
1965 -

ALINA
MOJICA
1965 -

KATHLEEN
HARTINGTON
KENNEDY
1951 -

JOSEPH
PATRICK
KENNEDY II
1952 -

ROBERT
FRANCIS
KENNEDY, JR.
1954 -

DAVID
ANTHONY
KENNEDY
1955 - 1984

MARY
COURTNEY
KENNEDY
1956 -

MICHAEL
LE MOYNE
KENNEDY
1958 -

m
1973

m
1979

m
1982

m
1980

m
1981

DAVID
LEE
TOWNSEND
1947 -

SHIELA
BREWSTER
RAUCH
1949 -

EMILY
RUTH
BLACK
1957 -

JEFFREY
RUHE
1952 -

VICTORIA
GIFFORD
1957 -

DIVORCED
1991

DIVORCED
1994

DIVORCED
1990

m
1993

m
1994

m
1993

BETH
KELLY
1957 -

MARY
RICHARDSON
1959 -

PAUL
HILL
1954 -

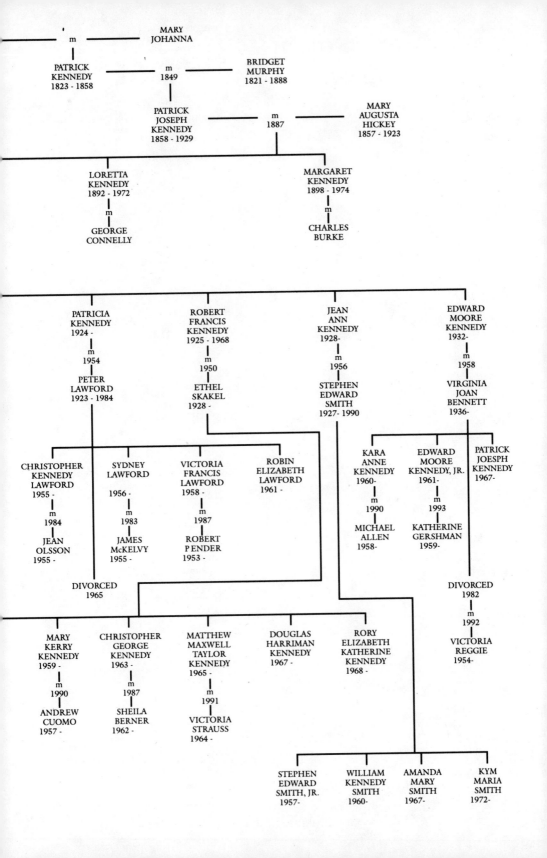

IRON ROSE

Rose Fitzgerald Kennedy
1890–1995

Excerpts from the eulogy
delivered by Senator Edward Kennedy

She was the granddaughter of immigrants who saw her father become the first Irish-Catholic Congressman from Boston and her son and grandson succeed him. She saw three sons serve in the Senate (actually, she was sure it was her campaigning that put us there, and we all thought that as usual she was right). She saw the son who proudly carried her Fitzgerald name become the first Irish-Catholic President of the United States.

And she was proud to see a new generation of her family carrying on her belief in public service.

But Mother also taught us that you don't have to run for office to make a difference. She was equally proud of her daughters and the contributions that they have made. Jean, the founder of Very Special Arts and now, like our father before her, the Ambassador. Pat, for the pioneering spirit she has given to young writers. Eunice, founder of the Special Olympics and the leader of a global revolution of human rights for the retarded and the disabled. And Mother had a special place in her heart of prayers for our sister Rosemary, for her bravery and the things she taught us all.

And most wonderfully, I think as I learned vividly from the past few days, Mother was an inspiration of faith and love to her grandchildren. As we gathered to share memories of Mother, grandchild after grandchild stood to tell anecdotes about Mother—different stories with one common theme.

She had instilled in the next generation the bonds of faith and love that tie us together as a family. She has left an incredible mark on our hearts and souls, and we are all blessed because of it.

Mother knew this day was coming, but she did not dread it.

She accepted it and even welcomed it, not as a leaving but as a returning.

She has gone to God. She is home. And at this moment she is happily presiding at a heavenly table with both of her Joes, with Jack and Kathleen, with Bobby and David.

As she did all our lives, whether it was when I walked back in the rain from school as a child, or when a president who was her son came back to Hyannis Port, she will be there ready to welcome the rest of us home someday. Of this I have no doubt, for as they were from the very beginning, Mother's prayers will continue to be more than enough to bring us through.

Introduction

It was 5:30 P.M. on January 22, 1995, and the reporters who were gathered in the dusk outside the Kennedy compound were bewildered. Each and every one of them understood they were witnessing a sorrowful event, but few could fully comprehend the enormity of the story they had been assigned to cover. Rose Kennedy was dying, and as she was 104 this was not a great surprise. But no one in the quiet crowd was prepared for the tremendous sadness surrounding Rose's family, a clan renowned for its bravery. Many members of the press sent out on this cold afternoon had been to the compound often before. But it had never been like this.

Most of those gathered were too young to appreciate the significance of Rose Kennedy, and the contribution she had made to the political formation of America although they had diligently reported news of her famous children and grandchildren. Now, for the first time, a stark reality hit home: Without Rose there would have been no Camelot, and twentieth-century America would have looked far different than it does today. Inside the compound, which stood silhouetted against the gloomy sky, each of the Kennedy family knew this, too. The woman who had inspired a dynasty was facing death.

Those gathered couldn't help but wonder if Rose's extraordinary life was, as we are led to believe in life's closing moments, now flashing before her. Did she reflect with pride on producing a son who became President . . . then suffer again the anguish of losing him to an assassin's bullet? Did she think of Bobby, and how he met his fate? Did she reflect on her girlhood in Boston, her Irish ancestors, her stormy, sometimes bitter marriage to Joe Kennedy? Perhaps in these last minutes of fading light, Rose thought only of her family en masse, an unstoppable force that she had molded, pushed, and willed to become a major part of American history.

This is the story of Rose Fitzgerald Kennedy, a legend known to millions but understood by few. It is an attempt to reveal the real Rose, a woman of courage in the face of disaster, a pillar of strength during times of our nation's deepest despair.

Part One

1890–1944:
Building a Dynasty

1

A Farewell in Boston: Rose Kennedy Dies at 104

"Fight the good fight."

It had been Rose Fitzgerald Kennedy's motto, and on this day 104 years after her birth, it was fair to say she had lived up to it. In spite of the tragedies, Rose had fought the good fight, she had kept the faith, and having lived until the age of 104 Rose had finished the course.

Rose Kennedy spent her last hours on earth surrounded, as always, by her family. As they gathered at her bedside, they began to accept the inevitable: The woman who had been their constant source of strength, who had led them through glorious triumphs and held them together through the most bitter of winters, was gone. She rested now in the palm of God, along with many other Kennedys and Fitzgeralds.

Rose had weathered many severe storms in her life-time, but even she could not overcome old age. Finally, the innocent deception the Kennedys had maintained for Rose over the past seven years was over, and nature had taken its course. For while the family had dutifully tried to keep things as normal as possible for Rose by dressing her, having her hair done once a week, and providing round-the-clock nursing care, in truth Rose had become a skeleton of her formidable former self. Unable to walk or to speak coherently, seeing out of only one eye, Rose found herself in a world that had dwindled to a single room within the Kennedy compound.

Home for Rose had become her ocean-facing, rose-colored bedroom, where she rested on a hospital bed equipped with rubber-clad safety bars. There she would pass the hours, interrupted occasionally by visits from family members. At times she would be taken downstairs in her wheelchair to sit in the sunroom or, when weather permitted, on the porch to stare at the ocean. Aside from photographs of her beloved children and their progeny, there was little to remind a visitor of the contribution this astonishing woman had made to twentieth-century America. Even Rose's most basic requirements for living had become greatly dimin-ished. Sadly, she had been unable to eat solid food since the end of 1980s. Instead, the matriarch who had once dined with the King and Queen of England and entertained at the White House was forced to spend the last six years of her life being fed via a tube to her stomach.

As her son Teddy, his wife, Vicki, and Rose's daughters—Eunice, Jean, and Pat—wept around her hospital bed, knowing what their mother's life had been reduced to in the end, they could console one another with the knowledge that they had all been dutiful children. Now Rose was moving on to a more peaceful place, where she would once again see her beloved husband, Joseph, and her three sons, Joe Jr., Jack, and Bobby, whom she had raised and watched as they were taken from her one by one. In heaven, too, would be her daughter Kathleen and her grandson David, along with the family's most recent loss, dearest Jackie, of whose death Rose was unaware.

The news of Jackie's death, which had transfixed the world in May 1994, never made it to the famous compound in Hyannis Port. Rose herself was ill as Jackie lay dying in New York. Although Rose recovered, she remained fragile. The family, fearing it might upset Rose, never passed on the news. It was a wise decision. There seemed little sense in adding unnecessary grief to Rose's final days.

Rose died only months after Jackie, but there was less pain for Rose and much more time to prepare. To a certain extent, at the age of 104 of course, the Kennedy family had been expecting it. Yet when the end came there was still a sense of shock, for they had nearly lost Rose many times before. Miraculously, she had always pulled through, and they hoped she would this time too. In the last few weeks of her life, however, Rose had failed badly, and the family was forced to face the inevitable. They wanted to make Rose as comfortable as possible, and during this period she spent her few waking hours watching carefully edited videotapes about her family. The triumphs and victories were all there, but none of the tragedy. There were no assassinations, no grandchildren dying from drugs or on trial for rape, no hint of Chappaquiddick and the other scandals that have plagued her last remaining son. Relinquishing the painful memories, she could truly rest in peace.

Just days before she died, Roman Catholic priests, who were regular callers to the Kennedy compound, came to give Rose her last rites. They arrived carrying a small box that held the oil and other necessities for the ritual, entered Rose's beautiful pink bedroom, and closed the door. Rose was already unconscious. Earlier, Teddy had felt compelled to make a heartbreaking decision, but in his view a humane one. People close to the Senator claim he had given orders that when his mother started to fail, there was to be no life support, no resuscitation.

It was not only at the compound that Rose Kennedy's death was felt. On this cold Sunday night a profound sadness seemed to shroud the whole of Cape Cod's southern shore and, by morning, to envelop the entire nation. The Kennedys' love affair with Hyannis Port began in 1925, when Joseph Sr. had rented what would become the Kennedy compound. Later in 1928 he bought the home for $25,000. On this day, seven decades later, rain poured from the skies above the tiny village, suggesting that even the gods knew this area would never be the same again.

Adding yet more sadness to the occasion were inescapable reminders of Rose in every corner of the house: the portrait of Joe Sr. that hung above the fireplace, the porcelain pieces scattered around the living room, the hundreds of photographs she proudly displayed of her family. This home was Rose Kennedy's pride and joy, and far more meaningful than bricks and mortar could imply. Rose had made it functional for her children, a safe haven from the stresses of political campaigns. In more recent years it became a place for younger members of the clan to gather and get to know one another. But above all it was the venue for the most important day of the year, July 22. That was Rose's birthday, the day when no matter what, the whole family would gather to pay their respects to the woman who had made it all possible. Tonight there was not a dry eye in this lavish home. Privately each Kennedy must have recalled Rose's last birthday party, and tried to imagine life without that yearly ritual. How would they all feel next July 22?

Teddy's face, wracked with grief, painted a picture that spoke for the whole family. It was almost impossible for his sisters Eunice, Jean, and Pat to look at him without crying. Yet while Teddy's sadness was expected, no one guessed that Pat Lawford would take the news as badly as she did. Two days later at the funeral, when scheduled to speak along with the other family members, the dutiful daughter could not bring herself to do so. She had lost her mother, and at this time in her life that cross was very painful to bear.

To each of her children Rose had meant so many

13

different things, but to all of them she had meant so much. Wandering around the compound those final days, lost in thoughts and memories, fighting the tears or giving in to the sorrow, each family member suffered a new kind of anguish. As one insider described it, "The compound had been a place for all sorts of occasions, but Rose had always been there as a pillar of strength. This made this time all the sadder."

It was a heart-rending end to a very painful week, which had begun when Senator Kennedy received word that his mother was experiencing breathing problems. The priest was called to administer the last rites. Despite her family's worst fears, Rose, who had proven so many times before to be superhuman, strong as an ox, appeared to rally over the next few days. She seemed to be faring so well that Teddy felt he could return to his work in Washington. Soon, though, his mother's health deteriorated. In many ways the sad turn of events was made worse by the absence of Rose's dear grandson, John Jr. Having been advised that his Grandmother's condition was improving, John postponed a visit to the compound. In the end he arrived only a short time before Grandma was pronounced dead.

Another member of the clan was noticeably absent, and had been for many years: Rose's daughter Rosemary. Her residence was in Wisconsin at St. Coletta's, a home for the mentally retarded. Here she lived a peaceful existence in her own quarters, known as the Kennedy cottage. Of all the things that had torn at

Rose Kennedy's heart throughout her lifetime—the loss of her husband, the deaths of her sons and daughter—Rosemary's mental retardation had been the hardest for her to come to accept. It made no sense in a family of such high achievement and privilege that one of its members would find everyday activities nearly impossible to handle. Yet Rose and all of the Kennedy clan had always tried to make sure Rosemary was included in family activities, and that she knew she was loved. On this night, Teddy dreaded breaking the news of her mother's death to Rosemary over the telephone.

Michael Kennedy, Bobby's son, was also absent. In keeping with an unfortunate tradition established by some members of this privileged family, Michael was battling an alcohol problem and had checked into a rehabilitation center just hours before. He too would be left remembering Grandma in happier times, as the lady who inspired them all.

It was 7 P.M. on January 22, 1995 when Senator Edward Kennedy shared the news of his mother's death with the world. The announcement was brief but spoke volumes about the depth of his family's love for Rose Fitzgerald Kennedy: "Mother passed away peacefully today. She had a long and extraordinary life, and we loved her deeply. To all of us in the Kennedy and Fitzgerald families, she was the most beautiful rose of all."

Rose was matriarch to more than a celebrated family of politicians. In a sense, she became the nation's matriarch as well. She played a vital role in shaping the political history of modern America, and it was fitting that some of the world's most powerful and famous people

15

came to pay homage to her in her final hours. On this night in the nation's capital, and especially in the Clinton White House, there was a sense of profound sadness and loss. "Very few Americans have endured as much personal sacrifice as Rose Kennedy," President Clinton said. "She played an extraordinary role in the life of an extraordinary family."

Back in Hyannis, locals spent the evening reflecting on the loss of their dear neighbor, a woman they had turned to for comfort during times of tragedy and uncertainty. Meanwhile, at the local hotel, the Tara, members of the media began to arrive. The next morning they would be up bright and early to get a glimpse of a family in grief. As the world came to terms with the news of her death, Rose Fitzgerald Kennedy was prepared for her next journey. At the compound that night she was dressed in her favorite rose-colored outfit, with appropriate matching jewelry and her rosary. It was time for her loved ones to say good-bye. The lid of her casket was closed and would remain that way for the following day's wake.

Monday, January 23, was a day of sorrow and reflection for all those gathered at the compound. Senator Kennedy spent much of his time making arrangements for the funeral, while John Kennedy Jr. got through this sad period by walking along the beach with his dog, Sam. From time to time throughout the day, members of the family could be spotted making their way along the wooden walk through the dunes to the beachfront, as they had done so often during happier family gatherings.

The compound at Hyannis Port had played a pivotal role in the history of the family. It was here that the clan learned John had been elected President in 1960. The compound had been the Kennedys' personal campaign headquarters, as well as a place for them to unwind and enjoy such pursuits as touch football and sailing—all the while honing the family image. But the house also resonated with painful memories. It was here that Jacqueline Kennedy had mourned the death of her infant son, Patrick Bouvier Kennedy. It was also here that in late November 1963 the Kennedy family grieved. That Thanksgiving, just days after the President's assassination, was the saddest day the family had ever known. During future times of sorrow, that occasion would never be far from anyone's mind. And so in mourning Rose, members of the Kennedy clan did what they had learned so well from sad experience: they comforted one another. Dozens of family members came to the compound at the end of Merchant Street to offer their prayers next to the casket. The mood was reflective, recalled one insider, "a time to prepare for the funeral and choose the readings and music that Mrs. Kennedy would have liked."

Even the local police chief, Neil Nightingale, appeared to shed a tear as he looked onto the house from his security headquarters at the top of the street, 250 yards away. He had witnessed many sorrowful moments here, and a number of happy ones, too. As always, he was joined by members of the media. There was the usual contingent of paparazzi, their cameras focused on John Jr. At one point a photographer was seen showing another media member the last photo taken of Rose on her deathbed. Even in death, there would be little peace for this much chronicled family. It was hardly surprising that the Kennedys often guarded their privacy fiercely.

Rose's wake was held in the rambling house by the sea. It was as private as any other Kennedy family occasion. No fewer than three priests from Our Lady of Victory officiated over the Roman Catholic Mass, which seemed appropriate for the woman whom many in the room felt was the most remarkable Catholic they had ever known. This last farewell to Rose was held in two parts, one in the afternoon, another in the evening, and visitors were allowed in by invitation only. Among those invited were many of the registered nurses who had helped care for Rose during the last difficult years of her life. These devoted people had played a vital role in keeping her alive by providing round-the-clock care from the time of her stroke in 1984, and the family wanted to make sure each of them had a chance to say good-bye.

Many of the assembled felt a special sympathy for John Kennedy Jr. and his sister, Caroline. During other times of grief Jacqueline had always been there to protect them, to buffer them from too much pain. Now Rose's two cherished grandchildren had to lean on each other. In many ways it seemed unfair that in their young lifetimes they had been forced to say good-bye to so many people they loved. But self-pity had never been in their repertoire. They learned at an early age that there was a high price to pay for being a Kennedy. It was a lesson Grandma had taught them: "To those to whom much is given, much is expected."

Monday, January 23rd 1995 had been a day for reflection. As each family awoke to watch the snow fall on Tuesday morning, they braced themselves for the final farewell to Rose. Today she would make her last journey back to Boston, her hometown. Some light relief came when Maria Shriver's husband, Arnold Schwarzenegger, lit a cigar and set off the smoke alarm, but aside from that there was little laughter. Quietly, the party prepared for the sixty-four-mile trek to Boston. The hearse, followed by cars and buses carrying the immediate and extended family, traveled the icy roads to Old St. Stephen's Church in the city's North End. En route, motorists stopped their cars and families huddled at rest stops to offer prayers. REST IN PEACE, ROSE read an electric billboard along Route 93.

Old St. Stephen's was the same North End church where Rose had been baptized more than a century earlier. The church even boasts a plaque commemorating her baptism there in 1890. Rose Fitzgerald Kennedy came full circle with this last trip back to the close-knit community of her youth. Unlike other members of the clan, Rose always regarded Boston as her home. While Joe Sr. made his name in New York and Hollywood (and could never quite forgive Boston for its snobbery and anti-Irish attitudes), and while her sons put their mark on the nation's capital, Rose was a Bostonian from start to finish. Such was her devotion to this city that many believed her husband's decision to move to New York nearly broke Rose's heart. Now the people of Boston returned the loyalty Rose had always felt for them. Many citizens helped prepare the church for the ceremony, volunteering their time to clean and repair the building. Several women washed the white pews, others polished the brass, and still others made sure the little church was resplendent with fresh roses. Even the organ, which hadn't received maintenance for almost a decade, was tuned.

Outside the church on Hanover Street, television cameras and satellite trucks grabbed their positions. Thousands of people lined the streets to bid farewell to Rose. As the cortege carrying Mrs. Kennedy pulled up outside, an eery silence fell over the crowd. A palpable wave of sympathy surged toward the family as they somberly entered St. Stephen's. John Kennedy Jr. and Arnold Schwarzenegger inspired the usual screams from some of the women in the crowd, but the organ music broadcast out onto the street was a sobering reminder that this was not a celebrity photo op, but a grave and historic occasion. The White House sent Tipper Gore, wife of Vice President Al Gore, and she was joined by a host of other political luminaries.

Inside the church, Senator Kennedy struggled to hold back tears as he delivered an emotional eulogy. "Mother not only gave to her children, but she gave her children, fired with her own faith, to serve the nation and earth," he said at one point. When he had finished, he walked to his mother's mahogany coffin, crossed himself, and then sat down and buried his face in his hands.

Rose had taught him not to cry in public. "I've learned to be brave and put my faith in the will of God," she once said. Indeed, Rose never shed a tear in public. Not when her eldest son, Joseph Jr., was killed in World War II. Not when her daughter Kathleen died in a 1948 plane crash, or when President John Kennedy was assassinated in 1963. Not when Senator Robert Kennedy was murdered in 1968, and not even when her husband died in 1969.

In fact, few people had ever seen Rose cry. Her former secretary, Barbara Gibson, remembers a day when Rose "happened to come into my office and see a telegram announcing the death of the Dallas priest who had given the last rites to President Kennedy. Ordinarily, I would have kept such news from her, in case it upset her, so I was distressed to see her begin to cry. Her sorrow touched me so much that I began to cry too. Almost immediately, Rose dried her eyes, looked at me coldly, and said, 'You must be tired, or coming down with something, to break down like that.' " But Gibson maintains to this day that Rose was angry only at herself, for showing weakness.

Yet even Iron Rose might not have demanded such composure from her children on a day like this. As daughters Eunice Kennedy Shriver and Jean Kennedy Smith and her beloved grandchildren addressed the congregation of over 800 people, their eyes were moist with tears. When the family made their way back to the cars and buses, John Kennedy Jr. seemed able to contain his grief only by comforting his sister, Caroline. Arnold Schwarzenegger spent his time looking after a visibly tearful Maria Shriver. And although Senator Kennedy's wife, Victoria, offered her main sympathy to her husband, her heart surely must have gone out to every member of the clan. Perhaps now she finally realized the enormity of what she had married into: a family whose most private moments of pain had to be shared with the world. A short while later, the group arrived at Holyhood Cemetery in nearby Brookline. Cardinal Bernard Law, the archbishop of Boston, said the final prayers, and Rose Fitzgerald Kennedy was laid to rest next to her husband, Joe, and behind her grandson David Kennedy.

Did Rose die with any regrets? We know of only one, a secret she wanted kept until after her death. Rose regretted that she had never become the first female President of the United States. Instead, she placed that hope and responsibility on the shoulders of another family member. As Rose's favorite grandchild, Caroline Kennedy Schlossberg, gazed at the family headstone, she had yet to learn of the task her grandmother had set for her.

Rose had made her confidant promise not to reveal her secret "until after I am gone." Once Rose was buried, however, that person felt released from that pledge. It was a vow made on a bright February afternoon back in 1985, at Rose's Palm Beach mansion on

Ocean Boulevard. There, Rose Kennedy confided that she had always yearned to run for public office. "If I had grown up in today's world," Rose declared, "without hesitation I would have become a politician." Then, after a short pause, she added, "Who knows, maybe I might have become the first woman President of the United States. Yes, I would have wanted that great honor."

It was hardly surprising that Rose, growing up in a family of politicians, would at one time have harbored political aspirations. But in light of the fate that had befallen her family, it was surprising that she would continue to voice that longing all those years later. Even more astonishing was the fact that she still felt public office was a pursuit worth the dangers, even for her disaster-plagued family. For while Rose realized that the times had been wrong for her, they were certainly right for younger Kennedy women.

On that winter day, Rose admitted that if she could not run herself, she wanted granddaughter Caroline to become the first woman chief executive. The conversation in Palm Beach that day went as follows:

"If it couldn't be you, would you like one of your grandchildren to become President, following in the footsteps of your son John?"

"Of course," replied Rose. "The family has always been politically oriented, and we discuss the presidency a great deal."

"Would you like to see one of your dozen girls, your grandchildren, make it to the White House as the first woman to preside over the nation?"

Without a moment's hesitation, Rose said, "Why, certainly."

"Would you tell me which one of your granddaughters would have the best chance, which one you would like to see in the Oval Office?"

Rose Kennedy pondered for a long moment. "Caroline," she said at last. "Caroline is the one who is best known, who would be the sentimental favorite. Remember that she was the country's pet during the administration of President Kennedy. She was his little 'Buttons,' who captivated the country. And wouldn't it be glorious to see little Buttons, years later, elected by the entire country to finish the job her father could not?"

At this point, possibly realizing the enormity of what she had revealed, Rose Kennedy caught herself. "Now, I don't want you to write anything about this. Not now. Not until after I am gone."

2

An American Irish Rose Is Born

A thousand years ago, Ireland's King Brian Bóru decreed that every family in the country must assume a surname. The name Kennedy, which meant "favored one," became a popular moniker. There were many times in her life that Rose Fitzgerald Kennedy would find it difficult to accept that translation. Her own family name meant "son of firm," and that's what the Fitzgeralds and their Rose would prove to be: firm and strong. In spite of everything.

Rose Fitzgerald was raised with a deep sense of history and ancestry. The plight of the Irish immigrant was told and retold by relatives who had lived it themselves, and she never forgot the deprivation they suffered in order to reach America. In turn, Rose made certain every member of her family honored the memory of that struggle, insisting that each of her twenty-nine grandchildren read Leon Uris's classic book *Trinity* so they would fully understand what had driven their forefathers out of Ireland. As Rose put it, "For my grandparents, it was the strength of their faith and the support of their families that gave them the courage to pull up stakes in Ireland in the 1840s and that enabled them to survive in the new world of hope and opportunity they found in America."

The Irish, Rose was taught, had faced turmoil on every front. In their homeland they battled not only the English but also famine and disease. America offered a means of escape, and every one of them who made it to the United States believed they had been blessed to take the journey. The voyage itself was fraught with danger. Across an often stormy Atlantic Ocean, immigrants endured forty days of appalling conditions, traveling in steerage. A good many of the 800-odd passengers who boarded these ships died en route, their bodies thrown overboard to the dark, roiling sea. The men, women, and children who remained suffered hunger and illness, and their cramped living quarters stretched emotions to the breaking point. Arguments routinely escalated into life-threatening clashes. Those fortunate enough to survive the passage consoled themselves with the belief that their very own pot of gold lay waiting for them on America's shores. If they completed the journey in one piece, they reasoned, it was because God had granted them the right to live. Armed only with determination and faith, they stepped onto American soil feeling, despite it all, quite lucky.

Rose's grandparents had made the transatlantic voyage in the 1840s, and Rose was named after her grandmother, Rosanna Cox Fitzgerald. Born on July 22, 1890, in the North End of Boston, Rose Elizabeth Fitzgerald was the first child of Mary and John Francis Fitzgerald. In those days the life expectancy of a woman such as Rose was 42 years.

Almost from birth, Rose Fitzgerald was in the spotlight. Her father was a second-generation immigrant, a street-smart politician who rose to the office of mayor while Rose was still a young girl. The Boston papers chronicled everything the Fitzgeralds did, and when Rose graduated from Dorchester High School—where she had been voted the prettiest and smartest girl in her school—her father, the Mayor, presented her diploma to her. It became front-page news. But despite the positive attention, Rose soon realized there was one group of citizens who wanted nothing to do with the Mayor or his daughter. These were the Boston Brahmins, the city's prominent, upper-crust Protestants, who considered the likes of the Fitzgeralds little more than low-class Irish. The Brahmins shunned the Irish for generations—a somewhat foolhardy practice, given that by the late nineteenth century Boston boasted more Catholics than Dublin. Their snubs would have a profound effect on Rose and her future family.

Despite a social climate that could be downright cruel, young Rose was certain of at least one fan: her father. By all accounts the girl adored John Francis Fitzgerald and was closer to him than she was to her mother. The feeling was mutual, and John's love and admiration for his firstborn sustained her as she grew to young adulthood. So close were the two that Rose would often take on the role of First Lady while her mother avoided the limelight. Mary Fitzgerald, unlike vivacious Rose, was a shy woman who said very little and ended up enduring long periods alone at home while her husband was out working—a scenario Rose herself would one day find replicated in her own life. For the moment, though, she was included in nearly everything. Unlike her siblings, Eunice, Agnes, John Francis Jr., and Thomas, Rose took an avid interest in her father's career, first when he was a local politician and later when he became Mayor of Boston. She was her father's helper and, to a certain degree, his confidant. Fitzgerald dubbed her "Princess Rose."

Those who knew him claimed that John Fitzgerald was a born winner. Everything he undertook went well, and he was a popular member of the community. John had come to politics by accident. After graduating from Harvard, he had been all set to embark on a medical career when his father died unexpectedly. Forced to assume the role of breadwinner in order to support his brothers and sisters (who now had lost both parents), John took on any job to keep food in their mouths, even dish washing. But he didn't have to struggle for long: Making money seemed to come easily to him, and soon he was able to accumulate a good deal of property. John's newfound wealth made him quite the eligible bachelor, and he quickly won the heart of elegant young Mary Josephine Hannon.

Fitzgerald won hundreds of other hearts as well in

his capacity as a politician. He had a way with people, a sense of compassion that other politicians lacked. It was a quality that earned him both respect and affection. To his constituents he was known as "Honey Fitz," a reference to the sweet effect his speeches had on the public. Certainly Rose found her father's voice soothing—for the most part. When it came, years later, to advising her prospective husbands, John's speeches were not nearly so supportive.

In Rose's formative years, however, their relationship was charmed. By the time she was two, Honey Fitz had become a state senator. From her earliest years Rose knew the way to her father's heart was through discussion. As she later remarked, "He talked to me incessantly when I was a child and young girl growing up, about everything in sight." Rose loved both her parents dearly and always credited them with shaping her character and ideals: "My mother and father instilled in me the same enthusiasm for life and thirst for knowledge that I am proud to see in my own children and grandchildren today. My father's love of public life could not help but be contagious, the way he made history and headlines come alive."

Although Rose was confident about her brains, she felt less secure about her looks. Young Rose, with her piercing blue eyes, did possess great beauty, but sometimes found herself enmeshed in sibling rivalry with her sister Agnes. The situation was only exacerbated when her father took both girls to the White House to meet President McKinley. During the visit McKinley remarked that Agnes was the prettiest girl ever to enter the building. No doubt the President meant only to flatter Agnes, not hurt her sister, but it did leave a lasting impression on Rose. From that moment on she made up her mind: Never would she play second fiddle to another woman, be it her sister, her future husband's floozies, or her sons' wives.

The most important meeting Rose Fitzgerald had as a young girl, however, was not with President McKinley but with a seven-year-old Joe Kennedy, whom she would later marry. The occasion was a Kennedy-Fitzgerald picnic in Maine at Old Orchard Beach when she was five, an event that would become a tradition over the course of many summers. Despite the two families' close ties, Joe Kennedy would one day have to move mountains to prove to Honey Fitz that he was worthy of his daughter's hand.

Joe, unlike Rose, was no hothouse flower, cultured and sophisticated and prone to scholarly endeavors. Young Joe Kennedy got his greatest education not from texts but from the mean streets of Boston. Joe's grandfather had been a skilled foundry worker, but like most Irish laborers he toiled long hours to make ends meet, often for little financial reward. Joe's father, Patrick, owned a tavern frequented by blue-collar workers. Young Joe was born in tenement surroundings and determined to escape them. Patrick Kennedy and Joe's mother, Mary Augusta Hickey, naturally shared their son's desire. Just like Honey Fitz, they realized that only with a top education might Joe—and future generations—defeat the snobbery and anti-Irish sentiments that pervaded Boston society. Joe's eventual escape came when he was admitted to one of the city's finest schools, Boston Latin. But his salvation did not lie in books. Instead, Joe focused on his wealthy classmates, scrupulously studying how to act and think the way they did.

Like Rose, Joe was rejected by the Boston Brahmins, whom he held in such high regard. Most of his contemporaries were poor, and their financial deprivation had made them tough. Sometime after the turn of the century, Patrick Kennedy became a City Councilman, which improved his social standing somewhat. Still, Joe's family could not give him much in the way of money or polish. The boy's only revenge would be to become as rich as the people who rejected him.

When Joe began his first term at Boston Latin, his family left their modest house and moved to a much larger home. They had saved their cash and were determined that Joe feel that his standard of living was at least roughly on a par with that of his classmates. Once enrolled in school, the young Kennedy immersed himself in extracurricular activities, namely sports and attempting to mix with the sons of prominent Bostonians.

This wasn't easy, for Joe was the only East Boston Irish boy at Boston Latin, and the other boys didn't let him forget it. Boston Latin, a prestigious institution established in 1635, counted among its famous alumni John Hancock, Benjamin Franklin, and Henry Adams. But the school also made a point of accepting boys from working-class families—if they exhibited the will to survive in the WASP world. These students, like Joe, were frequently reminded that they were outsiders, but nevertheless the education was invaluable. Attending Boston Latin would be useful to Joe in another way: It was the school John Fitzgerald had attended, and that would give Joe something in common with Rose's father.

Ever resourceful, Joe approached the class war at Boston Latin by turning his difference into an advantage. He determined to excel in sports, particularly on the baseball field. Joe Kennedy would prove he was indeed different from his classmates, and before he graduated many of the boys longed to be just like him. But if he was a breed apart from his upper-class school chums, Joe also had far outpaced most of his working-class boyhood pals. After graduating Boston Latin, he got accepted to Harvard.

Joe Kennedy was quickly becoming a very impressive young man. But there was still one document he needed in order to secure his future, and that would be a difficult negotiation for Joe: He needed a marriage license pledging him to Rose Fitzgerald.

While Joe Kennedy was storming the bastions of Protestant education, Rose was learning her own lessons about being Irish-American and Catholic. She had hoped to attend Wellesley College and had been accepted there, but her father refused to send her. Instead, she would attend the Convent of the Sacred Heart, a Catholic institution. Rose was dumbfounded and deeply disappointed with her father's decision. For the rest of her life she would regret not having attended Wellesley.

Rose learned a hard truth from the Wellesley fiasco: A woman's education was not her own to choose. Fortunately, this was not the only message about womanhood that Rose received from her family. Her mother, Mary, taught Rose just how essential a wife and mother was in shaping a family; it was a woman's devotion to her children, her intelligent attention to their individual needs, her guidance and steadfastness that created the very future of society. There is little doubt that Mary Hannon Fitzgerald had a profound influence on her daughter's character.

Aside from a deep devotion to home and family, Mary undoubtedly handed down to her daughter a legacy of thriftiness. Mary herself had only recently escaped humble origins, and she made sure her children understood the importance of a dollar. Rose clearly took these financial lessons to heart, for even after she had risen to millionaire status she was often accused of being stingy. Ever mindful of her ancestors' poverty, Rose always felt that wasting money was a terrible sin. "When I try to identify traits in myself," she once reflected, "I grew up with the idea that one should be careful with money, that none should be spent without good and sufficient reason."

She never lost her instinct for frugality. Throughout her life she saved money by turning out the lights, turning down radiators, and employing other tactics one might expect from a dollar-strapped wage slave, but never a Kennedy. For years Rose refused to heat the pool at the Kennedy home in Palm Beach. Instead, she'd swim at a friend's house to save money. On one occasion she even criticized Jackie for wasting water by taking too long in the shower.

If Rose's penurious reputation bothered her, she never let on. Perhaps one reason she clung so fiercely to her dollars was that she had not been to the manor born. She had relatives who were much worse off financially than she was: One of her brothers was a ticket taker at the Mystic River Bridge, and another lived in a trailer. They may have stood as constant reminders to Rose that not everyone was blessed with a fortune, and therefore one must be careful. To her credit, Rose always saw to it that her brothers, sisters, nephews, and nieces were not excluded from the Kennedy fortune.

Rose's ability to rise above or at least disregard ugly gossip was another skill she acquired early in life. At a tender age she learned that the press was intensely interested in the lives of the privileged and powerful—and that their interest was not always benign. When her father won the nomination for Mayor, Rose began to understand just how brutal news reporters could be. "I would wake up every morning to find my father accused in the headlines of being guilty of nearly every sin short of murder," she once recalled. Throughout her life, many of the stories Rose read about herself and her family were unkind; often they were untrue. But there were other occasions when news coverage of the Kennedys was not only awful but sadly accurate.

Ever since they were young children, Joe Kennedy and Rose had been friends. As Rose approached the end of high school, she became more and more attracted to the boy. She was entranced by his striking blue eyes, his hundred-watt smile. Joe was equally smitten with Rose, who was blossoming into a lovely young woman. While attending Boston Latin, Joe finally plucked up the courage to ask her to a school dance. John Fitzgerald promptly objected. Rose was baffled by her father's attitude: The Kennedys were a good family, the dance was being held in the afternoon, and above all Joe Kennedy was the best-looking boy she had ever seen. She soon got her wish to dance with Joe, at her high school graduation, but her relationship with the young man remained strained because of Honey Fitz's disapproval.

Rose's solution? The time-proven one used by lovers everywhere: She saw Joe behind her father's back. The two would rendezvous on street corners or at spots where she knew they'd be safe from Honey Fitz's eagle eye. They even met behind large dictionaries in the library. For a while the secret romance thrived, but a showdown was inevitable. It came when Joe asked her to be his date at Harvard's junior prom and Rose's father, either by coincidence or calculation, arranged a simultaneous family trip to Palm Beach, Florida. Naively believing she was in charge of her own destiny, Rose declined her father's invitation, but Honey Fitz lost no time in reminding his daughter exactly who was in charge. Even her usually reserved mother warned

Rose that she would be foolish to pass up such a wonderful opportunity to travel. Thus, a reluctant Rose made the journey to Palm Beach—and during every moment dreamed of Joe.

The trip, however, was not altogether dull. Rose was awestruck by the Florida island's exquisite beauty and staggering displays of wealth and power. She had never witnessed so much fame and fortune concentrated within a single area. Ironically, in future years Rose herself would become one of Palm Beach's most famous residents, along with the man she had left behind on this trip. The island would also be the scene of some of Rose's most heart-wrenching moments. Her grandson David would die of a drug overdose in this elite resort town, and another grandson, William Kennedy Smith, would stand trial there accused of rape. Palm Beach would play host to some of the more bizarre Kennedy-related dramas, and Rose would have a ringside seat at them all. It was considered part of her role.

At this stage in young Rose's life, however, Palm Beach simply represented separation from Joe, and that dampened her enthusiasm for the place. She could not understand her father's particular resistance to Joe, although she was aware that he would have found no man acceptable for his Rose—he had admitted as much to her on at least one occasion. "I was fortunate enough to have unusual advantages and opportunities, and therefore I shouldn't say yes to the first man who fell in love with me," Rose paraphrased her father, years later. "I should take my time and look around." The sentiment was endorsed by Rose's mother, but these reservations only confused the young woman. Here she was, dutiful daughter and devout Catholic, in love with an up-and-coming young man who was also Catholic. Why spend time seeking the affections of another? It made no sense. Honey Fitz went so far as to enroll Rose in a convent for a year, hoping to take her mind off Joe. Rose certainly did become more religious, she still could not forget Joe. Even trips to Europe didn't quell her desire. The indefatigable Rose learned to speak fluent French and German, but became even more strongly determined to be with the man she loved.

Eventually, Honey Fitz realized the absurdity of the situation. Not only was his parental protection hampering his daughter's yearnings, but he was beginning to see she could do a lot worse than Joe Kennedy, who by this time was earning a reputation as a prodigious businessman with a Midas touch.

While studying at Harvard, Joe had dabbled in the tourism business, investing in a bus. Upon graduation, he left for Europe and put money into real estate—a $1,000 gamble that turned into $25,000. Making money seemed an easy proposition for Joe. But with any investment comes risk, and even he was not immune. Soon Joe found himself $45,000 in debt. He devoted all his considerable energy to finding a way out of the red.

Joe got a lucky break in the form of nepotism. Because his father was politically connected, albeit on a local level, he was able to land a job as a state bank examiner. The position amounted to a crash course in banking, and Joe was a very quick study. Within a short time, he persuaded his father to let him take a shot at running the Columbia Trust Company, of which Patrick Kennedy was a director. Patrick believed that his hungry son just might have a recipe to turn the bank around, and his hunch proved to be correct. At 26 years of age, Joseph Kennedy became not only the country's youngest bank president, but also one of its most proficient.

For all the fuss Rose made over her courtship with Joe, years later she claimed not to remember how he had proposed to her. But the flawless two-carat diamond engagement ring must certainly have impressed the young woman. On October 7, 1914, as war raged in Europe, Rose Fitzgerald finally married the man she loved. The wedding was a quiet ceremony held in the private chapel connected to Cardinal O'Connell's home and attended by a few family members and some friends. Her sister Agnes was maid of honor, and the best man was John Donovan, one of Joe's Harvard pals. Joe wore a cutaway and top hat. Rose wore a Dutch cap of lace with an illusion net veil and a gown of rose-patterned brocade with a dropped waist and a long train. The future indeed seemed golden.

3

The Young Mrs. Kennedy

From the moment Rose became Mrs. Joseph Kennedy she realized that her husband had set extremely high goals for himself and his wife. Determined to break into the WASP world of high finance, Joe himself had evolved into a snob, extremely concerned about appearances and other people's opinions. This was most apparent in the young couple's choice of a first home. Other newlyweds might make do with a simple apartment, but not the Kennedys. Joe insisted they live in Brookline, a non-Irish suburb, and that they purchase a house. And so they moved into a home on 83 Beals Street, which today is famous for being President Kennedy's birthplace. On the day Rose passed away, its door was decorated with a rose-colored wreath.

Married life began smoothly enough for Rose and

Joe. The couple enjoyed a three-week honeymoon in West Virginia at the Greenbrier Hotel in White Sulphur Springs. By all accounts they seemed very much in love. During the day they took long walks together, and in the evening they played cards. Rose and Joe also pursued the other, most standard of honeymoon activities, and it was during this time that they conceived their first child. But Rose did not enjoy sex, and very shortly after this time conjugal exchanges would be reserved exclusively for the purpose of reproduction. After she conceived her last child, Teddy, Rose never slept with Joe again.

Home from the honeymoon, the newlywed couple moved into their seven-room house, which Joe had bought for $6,500, $2,000 of which he had borrowed. The rooms had been decorated while they were on vacation. They were finished in muted colors, the walls hung with reproductions of great paintings. As would be the case in their future homes, the living room was dominated by a grand piano that Rose and Joe had received as a wedding present. Ever mindful of their Irish roots, the china set used for tea was decorated with green shamrocks, a gift from Sir Thomas Lipton. The house at 83 Beals Street seemed to offer the perfect setting for a harmonious life together.

Their first few months of marriage were a bustle of activity. Rose was busy putting her personal touches to the home's decor, unaware that one day women from all over the world would come to examine her taste, which was simple and designed with children in mind.

Meanwhile, Joe purchased a car, a black Model T Ford, which once again set him apart from his more modest neighbors. Joe's main aim, it seemed, was to win the admiration of his peers in every arena imaginable. He had to be richer, smarter, a savvier businessman, an unflagging ladies' man. And so it would continue for the rest of the couple's long life together.

Joe promised himself he would be a millionaire by the time he was 35, and he intended to do whatever it took to make that happen. During the early days of their marriage, however, he also attempted to lead a normal life with his new wife. Together they would share friends and mutual interests. Rose, a lover of classical music, introduced Joe to it. He in turn shared with her his love of literature, his favorite author being Charles Dickens. Above all, though, they shared a desire to be parents, and as soon as they knew Rose was pregnant, their life was dominated by the anticipation of the baby's arrival.

In those days—it was 1915—most children were delivered at home. Rose delivered seven of her nine boys and girls in her own bed, attended by a local obstetrician with the cheerful name of Dr. Good. The doctor charged $125 per delivery, and Rose adored him. Joe and Rose awaited the arrival of their firstborn with near-religious fervor. Naturally, Rose was also nervous about the birth, and an army of help was hired to see her through this difficult time. By her account of the events, she gritted her teeth, put her faith in God, and took directions and encouragement from Dr. Good. As she later described it, "I tried to sublimate my discomfort in expectation of the happiness I would have when I beheld my child."

Joe, too, was anxious about his wife, and wanted to make her as comfortable as possible. To this end he rented a cottage in Hull, a pretty town by the sea near Boston. Joe believed the sea air would do Rose good. On July 25, 1915—just three days after Rose's birthday—she gave birth to a beautiful baby boy, whom they named after his father. From the very beginning both Rose and Joe Sr. were impressed by their visibly intelligent new son, and it wasn't long before they decided he was a leader in the making. The baby was big and strong and extremely healthy.

Rose took easily to motherhood. For her, like so many women, child rearing would prove to be the most difficult and rewarding challenge of her life. As she remembers in her autobiography, "I looked at child rearing not only as a work of love and duty, but as a profession that was fully as interesting and challenging as any honorable profession in the world, and one that demanded the best I could bring to it." Not long after Joe's birth, it became clear that husband Joe would spend most of his time away from home, pursuing his ever more ambitious career goals. On several occasions he was even absent when Rose was giving birth. But she seemed to take this in stride, accepting the deal they had struck: She would raise babies, and her husband would provide for them.

When his namesake arrived, however, Kennedy senior was still enchanted with the novelty of fatherhood.

He tried to spend as much time as he could with the bright little boy. In 1917 Joe took a new job as the general manager of a shipyard in Quincy, Massachusetts, and with the pressures caused by World War I, Joe's attention to his family trickled away. Eventually he seemed to come home only to sleep, and soon he had developed an ulcer. The war ended, but Joe's passion for work did not. He changed jobs again, this time venturing into the brokerage business. Ever the social climber, it was at this juncture that Joe befriended a man who would eventually provide him with the ultimate job. That man was Franklin Delano Roosevelt, then the Assistant Secretary of the Navy.

On the afternoon of May 29, 1917, Rose and Joe Sr. brought their second son into the world. They named the boy John Fitzgerald Kennedy, after Rose's father. While his elder brother Joe was the heartiest of lads, young Jack's childhood was marked by illness. Back then scarlet fever was a dreaded disease that often killed its young victims. Little John contracted a severe case when he was two. A terrified Rose believed her small son would surely die, and the doctors were not able to honestly assuage her fears. This horrible ordeal was the first major hurdle Rose was to overcome as a mother.

Little John's scarlet fever had given her the fright of her life, but there was worse to come. Rose could not have imagined the tragic illness her third child would have to endure, or the effect Rosemary's mental retardation would have on the Kennedy clan. It would be a sorrow that would haunt Rose forever.

Rosemary Kennedy entered the world on September

13, 1918, the same way her brothers had, at the family home on Beals Street. Initially she appeared to be a typical baby. Rose found her pretty daughter to be sweet, and she was certainly delighted by the fact that she cried less than the two boys had. Rose had a nurse to look after young Joe and Jack, so she was able to devote most of her time to raising Rosemary. Physically the little girl was quite healthy, and despite the fact that she crawled, stood, and spoke later than her brothers had, there seemed little cause for concern.

But as time went on, Rose became apprehensive about her girl's slow progress. When Rosemary seemed to take forever to learn to walk, Rose started to consider the possibility that her little daughter might be handicapped. Rose was heartbroken. Her job was motherhood, and here she was with a child who might not be normal. In her mind she had failed. Just how serious an avocation did Rose consider motherhood? Her autobiography, *Times to Remember*, makes her feelings clear. For her, being a good mother was a more noble achievement than writing a great book or painting a masterpiece. "What greater aspiration and challenge for a mother than the hope of raising a great son or daughter?"

While Rose agonized over Rosemary's health, Joe grew increasingly frustrated. Here he was, amassing a fortune and securing a very public place in the community, and one of his children was not capable of writing properly or participating in sports. To him it was infuriating, even shameful. Joe's children had to be better than everyone else's, and a daughter with below-average intelligence was not someone he could boast of to friends. Perhaps the most profoundly tragic aspect of Rosemary's life is that had she been born today, doctors might have diagnosed her with nothing more serious than dyslexia. But back then Joe and Rose's frantic efforts to discover what was wrong with their little girl—from consultations with Harvard experts to visits to America's finest hospitals—yielded no answers. As the years passed, Rosemary herself began to notice that she was being treated differently from her siblings. There was no question she was loved as much as they were, but she was rarely allowed to play the games they played. She had special tutors and struggled to keep up with her super-achieving siblings.

Rosemary's condition brought out the very worst in her father's character, inspiring him to commit an act of unimaginable cruelty. Taking the law into his own hands, Joe eventually issued what many regarded as his most ruthless command. It would also be the biggest secret he would keep from his wife. In 1941, Joe authorized the lobotomy of his oldest daughter. The operation would leave Rosemary, then 23, profoundly retarded and paralyzed on the left side. But Joe Kennedy did not want this attractive young woman with the childlike mind embarrassing the family—especially in light of the aspirations he had for his sons. Joe's decision would be just one of many that would break his wife's heart, but there is no doubt this one cut her the deepest.

Joe Sr. hurt Rose many times throughout their marriage. The first time Rose tried to do something about it was in January 1920, when she began to reflect on her life. She had long since come to terms with the fact that Joe spent most of his time away from home working. Still, after six years of constant child raising, she was beginning to feel isolated. Rose knew Joe was frustrated by Rosemary; he wanted winners, not losers. But there was more to Rose's growing despair than her disappointment with Joe's treatment of their daughter, who was still under their roof.

Rose loved her children for who they were. She didn't view them as trophies but tried to make them as well adjusted as possible. Yet this was a heavy task to undertake alone, and one weekend she decided it was all too much. Why should she have to spend so much time away from her husband? Why was her cherished Rosemary burdened with mental illness? Why couldn't her namesake enjoy all the hopes and dreams she had? Deeply anguished, Rose saw no way out but to run away. She hated Joe's lovemaking, hated the responsibilities of running a home alone—in short, Rose Kennedy hated her life. Maybe her father was right; she should never have married Joe.

And so Rose returned to her parents' home, hoping against hope they'd welcome her back. It was not to be. Her father's response was what she'd expected: "I told you so." But there was very little anyone could do to help. Rose was no longer a Fitzgerald; she was a Kennedy. "You've made your commitment, Rosie," Honey Fitz advised his favorite child, "and you must honor it now. The old days are gone. Your children need you, and your husband needs you. You can make things work out." With that, Rose knew she had no choice. It was back home to Joe, but this time on her terms. She demanded—and got—more help around the house. She demanded—and eventually got—a larger home for her family. Rose got, in fact, everything she needed, except a successful treatment for her treasured Rosemary.

While Rose continued to do everything she possibly could for Rosemary, she gave birth to a second daughter. Kathleen Kennedy was born on February 20, 1920, at the Beals Street house, which by this time was becoming overcrowded. As her family grew, Rose's mission—to raise healthy, morally upright, intellectually superior children—became more daunting. She decided early on that she'd need to keep a detailed record of each child. If her business was to be raising children, she would run it like a firm. To this end Rose kept index cards on each child. In later years, when Joe Sr. became Ambassador to the Court of St. James, the British press would compare Rose's efficiency to that of the Ford Motor company's production line. But index cards were the only way she could possibly keep tabs on her expanding brood. With the birth of each child, she recorded all the vital information—date and place of birth, church of baptism, and names of godparents. As her children grew older, she added other relevant details.

Rose made every effort to treat each child as an individual. "No child," she once said, "should be compared with another, for each has God-given potentialities which depend for full realization on influences in his or her environment." As supportive as she was, however, Rose was no slouch when it came to discipline. With such a growing family, the potential for chaos was ever present. Rose had no qualms about hitting her children when they were out of line, frequently using a wooden ruler or coat hanger to drive home her point. But any Mommie Dearest notions should be promptly dismissed. In later years her children would laugh at their mother's firmness, suggesting that "she would have made a good featherweight." It wasn't just manners that concerned Rose, either. She was particularly strict where money was concerned. From the age of five, each child was given a weekly allowance of ten cents. Rose was determined to teach every one of them the value of money, but alas, this accomplishment would elude her.

Rose did manage to instill in each of her children a strong sense of family. She spent as much time as possible with her boys and girls, and when there was a separation, they were never far from her mind. Rose could frequently be spotted walking along the streets of Brookline accompanied by three or four young Kennedys. She taught her children to stick together, which in many ways led to their being somewhat cut off from the outside world. Their clannishness (a term Rose despised) meant that the children became one another's closest friends. As Rose once confided to a reporter, "Years ago we decided that our children were going to be our best friends, and that we could never see too much of them." And this is what Rose and Joe did throughout their lives—they saw an awful lot of their children. It was a habit that would cause great friction for those who married into the family. Young Jacqueline Kennedy in particular could not understand why every holiday had to be spent with Jack's parents, every meal taken with a crowd of Kennedys.

Rose spent enormous amounts of energy on child rearing, a mind-boggling logistical feat that would earn her the respect of mothers around the world. Yet she expended very little outward emotion on her children. Or to the contrary, Rose Kennedy rarely showed emotion at all.

4

Rose's Solitary Confinement

Shortly after Kathleen was born, Rose's desire to move from the overcrowded Beals Street house was fulfilled. In 1921, parents and offspring found a larger home at 131 Naples Road, in an even nicer part of Brookline. Costing $17,000, the Kennedys' new abode had twelve rooms, and a veranda where the children could play, and was far more elegant than their previous residence. It was an appropriate setting for the family of a man who was beginning to prosper from his new ventures in the stock market.

In July of that year Rose gave birth to another daughter, whom she named Eunice, after her sister. From the first, Rose knew she had a bright child. In a rare diary entry on Valentine's Day 1923, the proud mother wrote of her eighteen-month-old daughter:

"Eunice walking alone and talking a lot. Best little talker of all." Rose was convinced Eunice would develop into a remarkable woman, and she was right: Eunice would one day make a name for herself helping the mentally and physically disabled by, among other things, founding the Special Olympics.

It wasn't long before Eunice was joined by a fourth sister, Patricia, and baby brother Robert. Rose Kennedy certainly had her work cut out for her. But while she could summon inner reserves of strength to deal with the challenges of her family and her role in their lives, the world outside posed a tougher dilemma. The fact was, she and Joe never quite fit in with the cream of Boston society, and it stung them badly. As hard as Joe tried—working all hours, making millions, and even buying a Rolls-Royce—he was still rejected by the WASP community he so desperately longed to join. Probably in response to the snub, Rose and Joe appeared to make a conscious effort to take the "Irishness" out of their children, although they still taught them to respect the traditions of their forebears. It wasn't that the Kennedys were ashamed—actually, quite the contrary—but they wanted their children to have access everywhere, and that meant blending in with the ruling elite. It was a very ambitious goal, but one that Rose and Joe would ultimately achieve.

Joe was fast amassing a fortune, though it is still not clear exactly how he did it. It's fair to assume that despite the introduction of Prohibition in 1919, Joe and his tavern-owning father did not interrupt their involvement in the liquor business. The revenues from sales of illegal alcohol, combined with Joe's investments in stock pools, apparently reaped huge sums of money. Joe was also able to profit from World War I by building and supplying ships to the Allies. He was helping the war effort, too—and all without actually having to fight.

But no amount of money could buy them into Boston's upper crust. The Kennedys would find that they were to be remanded to the outer circles of society, a fact rudely and irrevocably brought home to them in the summer of 1925. What should have been a wonderful family holiday turned into a bitter lesson in bigotry and dismissal for this nouveau riche but hardworking family.

After spending many summers in the predominantly Catholic Nantasket, where the Fitzgeralds had a summer home, Rose and Joe had decided to branch out and go to more fashionable Cohasset. Joe, the new millionaire, felt entitled to all the perks commensurate with his level of success, and membership in the local country club was high on his list of must-haves. But it took more than a fast-earned buck to gain entry to such a bastion of the Protestant upper class—as Joe and Rose learned when the members of the Cohasset Country Club turned their application down. The bar owner's son and the Irish Mayor's daughter were not welcome in Cohasset—though of course it was never stated in those terms. Joe, furious and humiliated, found this to be the last straw. He wanted nothing more to do with these people, who seemed to pull all the strings of Boston society. So he packed up his family and belongings and, determined to start anew in less socially constricted climes, booked a private railroad car to New York.

Rose was devastated by Joe's decision to move. Boston may have been snobby, but it was home. She was known there, her father was prominent and well respected, her friends and family were available to lean on when Joe was absent from the scene—which was most of the time. In New York she would be alone, and isolated. There was certainly no indication that Joe would suddenly pay more attention to his family after the move. He was out to reinvent himself: In New York he would show the world what the name Kennedy really meant. And as for Rose, she would have to survive.

After moving his family to New York, Joe decided to change courses once again. Always on the lookout for hot business trends, he was quick to observe what was happening on the other side of the country in Hollywood. Joe decided he wanted to be a movie producer.

His passion for the movie business had actually begun in another hot spot, Palm Beach, which had always fascinated him. This exclusive little island had everything: money, power, prestige. In 1926, while visiting the island, Joe came up with the concept of making low-budget movies. In the years to follow he would return with his movies and show them in the screening room of a house he rented on Clark Avenue.

But while these low-budget films were both popular and profitable, Joe had bigger dreams. He wanted big names and big box office. And a potential key to both came in the form of a stunning film star named Gloria Swanson.

Swanson was one of Hollywood's biggest stars and certainly one of its most beautiful women. The Chicago-born actress had already earned a million dollars by the age of 26, a hefty sum for any star in the 1920s. Her scandalous off-screen marriages only spiked the audience's fascination with her. Marriage No. 1, to actor Wallace Beery, took place while Gloria was still a teenager and proved as intriguing as any movie. When she became pregnant with his child, Beery gave her an abortion-inducing potion that not only killed the baby but nearly killed Gloria as well. Not surprisingly, the marriage failed. Things appeared to go from bad to worse when husband No. 2 took her for a million dollars in their divorce. The expression *third time lucky* did not hold true for Gloria either. She found herself a French Marquis, but then Joe Kennedy came along and made Gloria realize there was more to life than a European title.

Gloria Swanson was by any standards a huge financial success, but overbudgeted films and large divorce settlements had hurt her badly. Still, she had talent and earning potential, and a Paramount Pictures executive suggested she meet Joseph Kennedy, who was fast earning a reputation for making good movies and lots of money.

After much deliberation, a meeting was set up at the

Hotel Barclay in New York, and it was here that their mutual admiration society was formed. Gloria, who had suffered in the past from poor business advice, was absolutely smitten by Kennedy, the financial whiz. Joseph was equally dazzled by her beauty. Within a few days of their meeting, Joe had devised a plan to keep her from financial ruin. But his designs went well beyond the fiscal. And Gloria was all too ready to realize them.

Their affair began in the winter of 1928. It was the height of the fashionable season in Palm Beach, and Joseph Kennedy wanted a beautiful woman to share this spectacular time. Only one came to mind; he asked her to meet him. She agreed. Gloria boarded a train in New York and traveled to Florida, taking her husband, Henri, along for the ride—but Joe had other plans for him. As soon as her train pulled into the station and she saw Joe standing there with flowers, Gloria knew it would only be a matter of time before fate took its course. As she would later relate in her book, *Swanson on Swanson*, "I was standing in the doorway to the drawing room . . . when I saw Joe Kennedy come charging down the narrow aisle from the other end of the car like a cyclone. He pushed me back into the drawing room, said a few excited words and kissed me twice!"

For Joe Kennedy, eager to impress the people of Palm Beach, squiring around a famous movie star was a great coup. But he genuinely wanted Gloria for himself. Demonstrating an uncharacteristic flair for diplomacy, Joe dispatched Henri with dignity: He arranged a fishing trip for him, after which he gave him a job in Paris. Initially Henri was concerned that being apart from his wife would entice other men to chase her. But Joe assured his new employee that he would keep a watchful eye on Gloria. Later, the star was to recall just how watchful that was:

> He just stood there staring at me for a full minute or more before he entered the room and closed the door behind him. He moved so quickly that his mouth was on mine before either of us could speak. With one hand he held the back of my head. With the other, he stroked my body and pulled at my kimono. He kept insisting in a drawn-out moan, 'No longer. No longer. Now!' He was like a roped horse, rough, arduous, rearing to be free. After a hasty climax, he lay beside me, stroking my hair. Apart from his guilty, passionate mutterings he had still said nothing coherent. I said nothing at all.

The passion endured for two years, to be undermined by the very thing that had started it: business.

Joe's strategy for rescuing the star from insolvency had been to form a business partnership with her, called Gloria Productions. It was to involve, among other projects, an attempt to produce an epic entitled *Queen Kelly*—an ambitious film, to say the least. Production went on for months, and Joe invested at least $800,000 of his own money in it. Swanson, who was at the height of her career, was, of course, the star. Kennedy even hired the legendary Erich Von Stroheim to write and direct the movie. Von Stroheim had an awful reputation where budgets were concerned and seemed unable to grasp the concept of deadlines, but

Joe believed that his own business acumen would conquer all. He was wrong. The project collapsed before the film was completed. The *Queen Kelly* fiasco eventually led to Joe's ending his business dealings with Swanson—and the torrid affair they'd indulged in for two years. Their romance had ignited in the board room, progressed to the bedroom, and ended up on the cutting room floor. Rose Kennedy, meanwhile, was abandoned holding the babies.

Whether or not Rose knew her husband had fallen in love, she was pleased that her own brutally rough lovemaking sessions with Joe were over. She remained with her children, leading a life separate from her husband's and enjoying a separate bedroom. With the birth of Edward, her ninth child, on February 22, 1932, Rose deemed her marital obligations to produce children fufilled, and never slept with Joe again. But any notion of leaving was out of the question. Rose was Joe's wife forever, and no one would break that bond—not even a beautiful actress.

Her husband's friendship with the movie actress no doubt wounded Rose deeply. But her life was a complex one, and the suffering was relative. Was Joseph Kennedy's cheating more painful for Rose than their beloved daughter's mental retardation? Was Joe's spending weeks away from Rose, often in the company of beautiful women, more upsetting than the murders of two sons or the untimely deaths of two other children? It is possible that from the moment Rose's dear father ordered her to go back to Joe, she believed that whatever came her way was God's will. Yes, her husband hurt her, but for a woman like Rose there were few options, and so she steeled herself, held onto her life, and made the best of an unalterable situation.

It would have been nearly impossible for Rose to ignore the rumors of her husband's infidelities. The stories were not only muttered in private but also printed publicly. One Boston paper reported that Joe's transcontinental calls to Gloria in Hollywood generated the largest telephone bill in America in 1929. Sources also claimed that Joe was so besotted with Gloria "he begged her to have his child." As no child was produced, this has to remain conjecture. It is certain, though, that Rose must have known the husband she had tried to leave was involved with Swanson, and that he enjoyed showing off the actress to his friends and business associates.

Joe also wanted to show Gloria off to his family, a move that, astonishingly, Rose allowed. What effect Gloria Swanson really had on Rose will never be known. But in public she treated the movie actress in much the same way as she might have treated any of Joe's business associates—a point wonderfully illustrated by the way Rose wrote about the star in her memoirs.

"Obviously, the best adviser-manager-financier in Hollywood was Joe Kennedy," she wrote breezily. "I knew few of the details of his business ventures, whether buying or selling an office building, or stocks and bonds, or movie properties, but I do know Gloria wanted his advice and he did help to set her up as an 'independent.'"

To many this could be construed as hopeless naïveté on Rose's part, but she was no fool. Not long after Joe developed his friendship with Gloria, Rose became far more concerned with her appearance than she had been in previous years. "During Joe's years in the movie industry he was surrounded daily by some of the most beautiful women in the world, dressed in beautiful clothes," she stated. "Obviously, I couldn't compete in natural beauty, but I could make the most of what I had by keeping my figure trim, my complexion good, my grooming perfect, and by always wearing clothes that were interesting and becoming. And so, with Joe's endorsement, I began spending more time and more money on clothes." Suddenly Rose's frugality relaxed. Spending money in the interest of saving her marriage was a legitimate expense.

For the most part, though, Rose had her hands full raising Kennedys, with little help from philandering Joe. In future years he would reappear to advise his teenage sons, but initially it was Rose who reared them. Arranging her life completely around her youngsters, she slept with a notepad at her bedside so she could jot down any maternal detail she might remember in the wee hours of the night. "Whenever I held my newborn baby in my arms," she later recalled, "I used to think that what I said and did to him could have an influence not only on him but on whom he met, not only for a day or a month or a year, but for all eternity—a very, very challenging and exciting thought for a mother."

With the arrival of each new baby, Joe gave his wife

a present, perhaps to atone for the fact that he was often too busy to be at her bedside when she gave birth. When Jean Ann was born on February 20, 1928, Joe presented Rose with three diamond bracelets, from which she was to choose one. When asked by a friend what he would give her if she had a ninth child, Joe laughingly replied, "I'll give her a black eye." Despite the off-key humor, Joe realized he could not have picked a more devoted woman to mother his children. While he and his wife may not have been able to communicate sexually, in part because of Rose's deep connection to God, they shared a mutual devotion to family. Years later Joe would offer Rose this tribute: "I don't think I know anyone who has more courage than my wife. In all the years that we have been married, I have never heard her complain. Never. Not even once. That is a quality that children are quick to see."

There is no question that as a mother Rose left little room for criticism. She did a valiant job of balancing her life around nine little individuals, each with his or her own hopes and dreams. She certainly had staff to help her and enough money to employ more, but Rose preferred the hands-on approach—it suited her appetite for efficiency and control. Each morning she awoke, went to Mass, and was back at the breakfast table to join her children for the first meal of the day. Although Rose's devout Catholicism bordered on martyrdom, she made sure that the religious instruction her children received was of a more balanced nature. She took the young Kennedys to church every day, and after Sunday Mass she discussed the service with them;

beyond that, however, she didn't push it. Rose believed that the Catholic faith gave them a sense of responsibility and security. She was right: In later years it would provide a haven for them, a buffer from the trials they would endure individually and as a family.

Rose also encouraged outdoor sports for the children, games that would keep them fit and healthy. She made sure they all attended dancing classes and took golf and tennis lessons. At a very young age they were taught to swim and ski and, when they were old enough, to sail. While not a keen sailor herself, Rose wanted her children to learn to master it.

Mealtime was a focal point in the Kennedy household. Rose felt it was very important that the whole family gather to eat. A strict schedule was kept: Lunch was served at 1:00, and dinner at 7:15, except for the younger children, who ate an hour earlier. The dinner table provided an arena for discussion, and Rose made sure each child had enough to talk about. One visitor would eventually tell writer Gail Cameron that there were definite prerequisites for a visit to the Kennedy home, rules that Joe Sr. was fond of reciting to guests prior to dinner. "Prepare yourself by reading the *Congressional Record, US News and World Report, Time, Newsweek, Fortune, The Nation, How to Play Sneaky Tennis,* and *The Democratic Digest.* Memorize at least three good jokes. Anticipate that each Kennedy will ask you what you think of another Kennedy's (a) dress, (b) hairdo, (c) backhand, (d) latest public achievement. Be sure to answer, 'Terrific.' This should get you through dinner. Now for the football field. It's touch, but it's murder. If you don't want to play, don't come. If you do come, play, or you'll be fed in the kitchen and nobody will speak to you. Don't let the girls fool you. Even pregnant, they can make you look silly. If Harvard played touch, they'd be on the varsity." And so the list for surviving a Kennedy gathering went on. But if it seemed demanding for a guest, it was even more difficult for a member of the family, especially with Rose in charge.

The tempo slowed not a whit on vacations. During the summer Rose compiled reading lists in order to keep her offspring busy. Mealtime schedules were rigid as always, and anyone who attended late was reprimanded. While her youngsters were given every advantage, they were hardly indulged. If they wanted to buy a new toy or book, they had to save their money. If their bicycles broke, they had to fix them. To keep up with every detail about each child, Rose ran a very, very tight ship. Whether she ever considered how her skills might have been put to use in a business other than running a family we will never know, but it is abundantly clear that Rose put her children first and took great pride in the job of motherhood.

Over a period of seventeen years, from 1915 to 1932, Rose Kennedy bore nine children. The oldest, Joe Jr., always the apple of her eye, was raised to be head of the family. From the moment he was born it seemed clear that Joe was a special child. Bright and happy-go-lucky, he was quick to smile and laugh and joke. No doubt about it, young Joe had all the leadership qualities Rose and Joe Sr. had dreamed he would.

He was a lot like his father—self-assured and aggressive. They expected great things from their son, and he tried hard to please them.

Joe Jr. was no angel. Like all children he got into mischief, especially with his younger brother, Jack. Their boyhood fights blossomed into an extended rivalry once they entered school, which may have been inevitable given the excruciatingly competitive climate of the Kennedy home. The bond between the brothers was strong, however. They attended the same schools, and because they were Irish-Americans they learned to stick together. Jack had a high IQ, but his schoolwork paled next to his older brother's, and that hurt. Since they were Kennedys, their rivalry was not only intellectual but also physical. Occasionally their roughhousing got out of hand, and Rose would have to call Joe Sr. in order to calm them down. But Rose was the first to accept that brothers with only a two-year age difference would be prone to fight and argue.

As Joseph Kennedy became richer, the Kennedy lifestyle grew proportionally more lavish. Yet the children remained oblivious of just how much the family was worth. "We never gave them allowances that were any bigger than those of the neighborhood children," declared Rose. "We never put value on anything just because it was expensive. Nobody talks about money in Boston, and we made it a rule never to speak about money in our house." But the Kennedy children were indeed different from others in the neighborhood. Each of them would be worth over one million dollars by the age of 21. According to Kennedy historian John

H. Davis, "Joseph Kennedy did a remarkable thing. He had made a lot of money but he had no intention of hoarding it. He knew that if his children were to enjoy a high and secure social position someday, they had to have money of their own. Accordingly, he set up trust funds from which they would start receiving incomes at the age of 21." Liberated economically, the young Kennedys could be free to explore any career they chose.

Rose was a facilitator in the liberation of her children, acting as trustee, but she never enjoyed liberation of her own. Instead, she lived vicariously through each child. When Joe Jr. got accepted to Harvard, it somehow vindicated her own not attending Wellesley. When Jack was elected President, that victory somehow enabled Rose to fulfill her own political ambitions. When Kathleen entered the British aristocracy by marrying the Marquess of Hartington, it symbolized, finally, an acceptance into high society. Sadly, this heightened emotional investment had a darker side than any parent can bear. When Joe Jr. died in action in World War II, part of Rose surely died with him. When Kathleen perished in a plane crash, another part of Rose went down with the wreckage. And when Jack was assassinated, Rose would die yet again. Rose's only constant would be God; He remained with her throughout and asked nothing in return.

Rose made her nine children the center of her universe, but for the most part she lived her life unsure that they would return the devotion. She once confided in her secretary, Barbara Gibson, "You know, it's funny. You would cut your arm off for your child," and then she paused for a moment, "but you would do nothing for your mother." A strange and sad reflection coming from one who had raised a family so single-mindedly and so well.

In many respects, of course, Rose had much to be happy about during the 1920s and '30s. A virtually limitless pot of money was at her disposal, and she had top-notch help running her beautiful homes in New York, Hyannis Port, and Palm Beach. Of all the Kennedy abodes, none had a stronger pull on the family than their summer house at Hyannis Port.

Having been rejected by the WASP community of Cohasset, it was important for Joseph Kennedy to establish a summer residence where he and his family would receive the respect he believed they deserved. Cape Cod's southern shore was fast becoming fashionable in the mid 1920s, and after taking a couple of summer rentals there, Joe and Rose agreed that the area felt perfectly comfortable. Joe bought a house for $25,000 that was in desperate need of remodeling. Already more than twenty-five years old, it was duly repaired and enlarged to accommodate their ever increasing family. Rose was adamant that the Hyannis Port home never look overly decorated or too precious. She wanted a comfortable retreat for her children, not a museum. Hyannis Port would prove to be a great training camp in creating the Kennedy clan's moral fiber. There they would learn to interact, play together, study together, and above all stick together. As one source put it, "Forget playing football with them; they only pass the ball to a Kennedy."

Rose came into her own in Hyannis. She adored the local church, St. Francis Xavier, and went to Mass there every day. Rose also attended the local theater. But most of all, Hyannis was the place where Rose rediscovered solitude. When the children became too much for her, she could slip away to a cottage on the compound and be alone with her thoughts. She loved to walk and could frequently be seen strolling by herself along the Cape Cod shore. In Hyannis, too, Rose developed a passion for golf.

While Hyannis Port would become the Kennedys' summer retreat, winters eventually were enjoyed in Palm Beach. The island offered Joseph Kennedy everything he so desperately craved—good breeding, wealth, power, and privilege. The stock market crash of October 1929 saw great fortunes lost overnight, but Joseph Kennedy's money was only slightly affected by the disaster. A few years later he was able to clean up in Palm Beach. The house on 1095 North Ocean Boulevard was just the sort of property for which he was looking. It had been built in 1923 by famed architect Addison Mizner for just under $50,000. Its owner, Rodman Wanamaker, a victim of the crash, needed money, and in the early 1930s Joseph Kennedy was one of the few people who had any left. In 1993 Kennedy bought Wanamaker's home for about $100,000 and then paid another $15,000 for the lot next door in order to maintain his family's privacy. Equipped with a pool, tennis court, an underground tunnel to the beach, and six large bedrooms, the house provided Rose and Joe with an ideal winter getaway.

It would also prove significant historically. John F. Kennedy stayed there during his convalescence from back surgery in 1954–55, and as the newly elected President in late 1960, he made it his headquarters before the inauguration. Joe Kennedy's favorite spot on the property was the Bull Pen, a white-fenced enclosure near the swimming pool where he could sunbathe nude and talk on the telephone. For Rose, the house was a symbol of having, at long last, arrived socially. Now the same people who had rejected her would gaze in envy at her splendid home. It's not surprising that after Rose's death there seemed little reason for the family to keep the house. And so in April 1995, just three months after Rose was buried, the Palm Beach compound was sold.

5

Ambassador Kennedy and Rose

Joe Kennedy spent the 1920s expanding both his empire and his family. Later he turned his ferocious energy most of all to his sons, Joe Jr., Jack, and Bobby. By the 1930s, the time was right for Joe Sr. to begin paving their way to greatness.

He shrewdly began this campaign by trying to help those who in turn might help him. In 1936 Joseph penned a book (with journalist Arthur Krock) that he hoped would become a bestseller: *I'm for Roosevelt*. It gained him loads of attention—from everyone but Roosevelt. According to Kennedy historian John H. Davis, "When Joseph sent Roosevelt a copy, initially there was no response—Roosevelt was up for re-election that fall and was terribly busy. Angry and hurt, Kennedy urged the president's secretary to try to get a written response from her boss. Finally, to Kennedy's immense relief, it came."

Dear Joe,
I'm for Kennedy. The book is grand. I am delighted with it.

Yours sincerely,
Franklin

The letter and the book would forever stay dear to Joseph's heart, but *I'm for Roosevelt* contained some out-and-out lies. The most noticeable referred to Joe's own plans and those he unquestionably had for his sons. "I have no political ambitions for myself or for my children," he stated. Nothing could have been further from the truth. He had grand ambitions for both himself and his children, and believed this show of support for Roosevelt would get him a job within Roosevelt's new cabinet. Joseph Kennedy was wrong, but only temporarily. Another man's illness eventually provided the opening Kennedy desired, boosting him and Rose one rung higher on the social ladder.

To this day no one fully understands what President Roosevelt was thinking when he appointed a staunch Irish-American Catholic to be Ambassador to the Court of St. James. But when Robert Worth Bingham, then American Ambassador to Britain, took ill and was forced to return home, Roosevelt had to find a replacement. The President was well aware that Joseph Kennedy wanted the job, and in many ways Joe deserved it. He was not only a successful businessman but also had demonstrated genuine concern for the country. He had certainly shown his loyalty to Roosevelt, not only by writing the book but also by contributing hefty sums to the President's campaign efforts. Usually ambassadorships are handed out to longtime chums of the President; in this instance that was not the case. In the eyes of many Americans, this made Kennedy an appealing choice for the position.

In late February 1938, Joe set sail for London, with Rose and the children following on March 3. A crowd of friends and members of the press turned out to wave good-bye to the Kennedys. It wasn't Rose's first trip to Europe, but much had changed since she had accompanied her father there as a young woman.

Rose was nervous but thrilled about her new role as Ambassador's wife. The British press eagerly anticipated the arrival of this much-talked-about—and sizable—American family. Rose later remembered those days with affection: "The British press seemed fascinated by the idea of a large and lively Boston Irish family descending on the London diplomatic scene. There had already been a good deal of advance publicity about us, and once there we became practically public property. I almost began to feel that we had been adopted, as a family, by the whole British people."

It seemed that everywhere the Kennedy family went they were greeted by cheers of joy. Within two days of their arrival in London, Rose and Joe were received by the Queen at Buckingham Palace. Rose was enchanted by the introduction. "She had such a happy, natural smile and friendly manner," Rose remembered, "that I felt at ease with her at once. She indicated I should sit beside her on a small sofa near the fireplace and that Joe sit in a big, comfortable-looking chair opposite us."

The Queen (now the Queen Mother) and Rose would enjoy many conversations. They had much in common, especially love for their children. Her daughters, princesses Elizabeth and Margaret, were about the same ages as Jean and Bobby. Rose was fascinated to hear the Queen's stories about them. It wasn't long before she and Joe received another invitation into the royal circle.

Meanwhile, however, the mundane chores of everyday living had to be handled. Relocating an entire family across the Atlantic was not an easy task, especially when carried out in full public view. The exercise was made even more challenging by the fact that the Ambassador's residence at 14 Prince's Gate had only eight bedrooms to house a family of eleven. Although it once had been a luxurious residence, time and the wear and tear of previous owners had taken their toll. In typical fashion, though, Rose rolled up her sleeves, dove into the mess, and set about creating a home in which she could entertain London's highest society. Here Joe's wealth proved indispensible. Because while he earned $17,500 a year as Ambassador, he would spend at least $250,000 annually during his stint in England. It was assumed that U.S. Ambassadors would greatly supplement their salaries with their own cash. Being rich, in fact, was an unspoken prerequisite for the job.

In England Rose no longer sat home waiting for her husband to grace the family with a visit. She was expected to accompany him everywhere. It was like making her debut all over again, only on a bigger and better scale. Frequently she thought of the society WASPS she had left behind in Boston—and how she, who had been rejected by the Brahmins, was now welcomed at Buckingham Palace. Perhaps Rose's greatest social triumph came when she received a royal invitation to Windsor Castle, where other guests included then British Prime Minister Neville Chamberlain.

Son of a previous Prime Minister and leader of the Conservative Party, Chamberlain was deeply committed to the policy of appeasement as a way of dealing with the threat of Nazi domination of Europe. Joe Kennedy would eventually come to defend Chamberlain's stance, even after the Prime Minister's meeting with Hitler in September 1938, a move frowned upon by most of the British population. While many condemned Kennedy's support of Chamberlain, it should not necessarily be construed as an act of support for Hitler. Both men hoped to avoid war—a mission at which they both failed. Chamberlain and Kennedy would soon realize they had underestimated the beast. And as a result, both men would find themselves guilty by association.

For the moment, though, the talk in the American Ambassador's household was not of war, but of what to wear to Windsor. Rose had quickly learned to take her design direction from the British—a most diplomatic approach. For jewels, Rose managed to borrow a tiara.

The weekend at Windsor Castle was one of the most

fascinating Rose had ever experienced. Aware that this was a special occasion of magnificent proportions, she kept a play-by-play account of the weekend in her diary for posterity. In her memoir, *Times to Remember*, she carefully chronicled the grand introduction the Kennedys received, escorted by footmen to be presented to the King and Queen. The ladies curtsied and the gentlemen bowed, after which everyone followed the royals into the dining room—unquestionably one of the grandest in the world. Here, for the first time, Rose fully comprehended the weight of history that surrounded her. On the wall behind the Queen was a portrait of Queen Victoria. As a young girl, Rose could never have imagined that she would one day gaze at this painting while sharing a table with one of Victoria's relatives. She also realized that if she had left Joe or forced a confrontation with him about Gloria Swanson, neither of them would be in England dining in such company, and certainly not as Ambassador and Mrs. Kennedy.

The Queen and Mrs. Kennedy seemed genuinely fond of one another, a reality that even mystified Rose: "I lay in bed thinking I must be dreaming that I, Rose Kennedy, a simple young matron from Boston, am really here at Windsor Castle, the guest of the Queen and two little princesses." When Rose felt ill at ease addressing her new friend in the appropriate fashion, namely as "Ma'am," the always gracious Queen insisted it was not necessary. It certainly seemed that within the first few months of her arrival in England, Rose Fitzgerald Kennedy had won the royal seal of approval.

Rose regarded Britain as a wonderful place in which to show off her daughters—even Rosemary, whom Rose always included in everything. During the first few months after their arrival, Kathleen and Rosemary had a joint debut. All in all, the Kennedy clan was fitting into London very well. Rose took in tennis at Wimbledon and racing at Ascot. The truth was, Great Britain offered Rose a chance at reinvention. She was taken at face value, recognized as the Ambassador's wife. Wherever she may have come from, whatever schools she may or may not have attended didn't matter any more. For the first time in her life, she was really enjoying being married to Joe.

While Rose's self-esteem may have been boosted in Britain, the new location didn't diminish her dedication to her children. As always they remained her primary concern, and she continued to keep notes on each of them. Entries in her diary during this time included the removal of Teddy's tonsils and a record of Kathleen's hunt for a college. On the surface, life puttered along as usual for the clan. But behind it all lay the backdrop of a darkening Europe, the threat of Hitler, and the knowledge that whatever Joseph Kennedy suggested to the President might have a vital impact on the future of the world.

Although Rose and Joe made great strides socially those first few months in England, that certainly wasn't their prime reason for being there. Joe's capability in his role as Ambassador was the larger issue. His posting, which began in March 1938, got off to a good start. One insider recalled that "the regular diplomats were absolutely terrified of Joe," but "the press went absolutely ape over the entire family. I don't think there was a day in the month that there wasn't a photograph of the Kennedy family." As popular as the Kennedys were, however, Joe's political views would end up earning the clan mixed reviews. In fact, of all the mistakes Joseph Kennedy made in his lifetime, it's fair to say his biggest may have been to underestimate the British—and to be both undiplomatic and outspoken about it. But then Joe had always been a contradictory man, one who made up the rules as he went along. He hated the upper class but aspired to belong to it. He believed in family but usually spent more time increasing his finances than nurturing his brood. He appeared to love women but often treated his wife miserably.

Joe was confident he had the right to behave exactly as he pleased, no matter where he was. The upper-class British were not impressed. No Ambassador to the Court of St. James had ever arrived with his own public relations man, but Joe had brought Harold Hilton, who busily offered up stories about the Kennedy family, as if the purpose of Joe's position were to promote the clan rather than to represent America. As it turned out, Joseph would indeed require a PR man—not for promoting, but to salvage his image.

Despite his wealth and apparent sophistication, Boston-bred Joseph Kennedy was in many ways out of place in London. Blissfully occupying his new position of power, Joe seemed remarkably insensitive to the

British sense of decorum. He was quick to win the public over, an art the Kennedys have mastered to perfection, but the elite found him offensive. The president of the Bank of England called him "a man permanently on the make." Even the Queen, who had a lot of time for Rose, must have shuddered when she was told that the Ambassador often greeted people in his office with his feet on the desk, that he chewed gum, swore profusely, and frequently lost his temper. The Queen would also learn that Kennedy allegedly described her as "a cute trick." Whether Kennedy actually said this cannot be confirmed, but it is generally acknowledged that while Rose behaved charmingly, Joe was often coarse and common. He would remain a social outcast.

Kennedy had plenty of detractors in London. Sir Henry Cameron wryly remarked that "his chief merit seems to be he has nine children." Harold Ickes, in one of his diary entries, made reference to a statement made by a member of the Wedgewood family: "At a time when we should be sending the best that we have to Great Britain, we have not done so. We have sent a rich man, untrained in diplomacy, unlearned in history and politics, who is a great publicity seeker and who is apparently ambitious to be the first Catholic President of America." Another esteemed gentleman was even less flattering toward Mr. Ambassador. Lord Francis remarked that Kennedy was "a tycoon who seemed to me when I met him to combine all the disagreeable traits of all the very rich men I had ever met with hardly any of the virtues."

The Establishment's dislike of Joe could be dismissed as silly bickering, but Kennedy's actions and attitudes, unfortunately, affected far more than just the society pages. Hardly a few hours before Hitler's troops invaded Vienna, Kennedy wired Roosevelt to say he believed Hitler was bluffing. Yet when the Germans began to bomb London, Joseph walked in Green Park, looked over toward Buckingham Palace, and said, "I'll bet you any sum, at odds of five to one, that Hitler will be sitting there in two weeks." Kennedy apparently knew little of the resilience or determination of the people in whose country he was residing.

While Joe was a keen defender of the Kennedy name and image, he seemed to have little compassion for others. When Hitler threatened to invade Czechoslovakia, Joe declared publicly, "I can't for the life of me understand why anyone would want to go to war to save the Czechs." Even more alarming was his response when Neville Chamberlain returned from Berlin after capitulating to Hitler's demands. Chamberlain announced on his return to London, "I believe in peace in our time." Joe Kennedy's reaction was, "Now I can go off to Palm Beach."

One Englishman did stand up and speak his mind. Winston Churchill fully understood what Adolf Hitler was all about. He also knew that unless something was done to stop him and his storm troopers, havens like Palm Beach would become entirely irrelevant. More important, he felt that racial hatred could not be tolerated. Churchill was everything Kennedy would never be: aristocratic, honest, statesmanlike. As soon as Chamberlain returned, Churchill responded by addressing the House of Commons in a radio broadcast that was heard by the British and American people alike.

> Is this a call to war? Does anyone pretend that prepara-
> tion for resistance to aggression is unleashing war? . . . I
> declare it to be the sole generator of peace. We need the
> resolute and sober acceptance of their duty by the English-
> speaking peoples and by all nations, great and small, who
> wish to walk with them. Their faithful and zealous comrade-
> ship would banish from all our lives the fear which already
> darkens the sunlight to hundreds of millions of men.

Joseph Kennedy was free to enjoy Palm Beach, but any hopes he had of becoming President were dashed forever. On September 13, 1939, President Roosevelt was asked by an intimate how Kennedy was getting on as U.S. Ambassador in Great Britain. "I want to tell you something," Roosevelt confided, "and don't pass it on to a living soul. Some weeks ago Joe had tea with the King and Queen, who were terribly disturbed about the war situation. Afterward he saw Samuel Hoare and several others. . . . After his talks Joe sat down and wrote the silliest message to me to do this, that, and the other thing, in a frantic sort of way." Kennedy, Roosevelt continued, had been "taken in" by his acquaintances in the British government and royal family. He could therefore not be relied upon for the most solid of judgments.

On September 3, 1939, Rose, Joe, Joe Jr., and Jack turned on the radio to hear Neville Chamberlain declare war. "Everything that I have worked for, everything that I have hoped for, everything that I have believed in during public life has crashed in ruins," Chamberlain lamented. Later that day as sirens wailed through the city, Rose found herself running with her two boys down the panic-ridden London streets. Joe Kennedy's millions meant little to her now; she only knew she had to take her children and leave.

On September 18, 1939, a grim and tired Rose boarded the *SS Washington* with Kathleen, Eunice, and Bobby. Rosemary stayed on to complete her schooling. Joe Sr. was to remain in Britain for just over a year. The crammed quarters housed 1,800 passengers, and Rose frequently thought about the plight of her ancestors during the journey home. She had much more to look forward to when she arrived than they had, but the voyage was so difficult there were moments when she wondered whether she'd arrive intact. Yet arrive she did, just in time for the golden wedding anniversary of her parents.

Communication between Rose and Joe was limited by the war. Transatlantic phone calls had to be kept to a minimum, so they decided to keep ten minutes open every Sunday so Joe could speak to Rose and all the children. At this point, his family were probably the only ones keen to speak to Joe Kennedy. Just as Joe's endorsement of Chamberlain had proved a large mistake, so was his failure to recognize Churchill's power. Ultimately, Roosevelt became so embarrassed by his envoy he called him home. Out of favor with his own President and, persona non grata with the British,

Joseph Kennedy's tenure as Ambassador ended in humiliation.

During that final year in London, before Roosevelt called him back, Rose remained loyal to Joe. In addition to the weekly phone calls from their house in Bronxville, outside New York City, she wrote to her husband. Her letters offered more emotion than he had received from her in years: "My darling— I am wondering when I shall see you and what is happening! It is all so heartbreaking." She wrote of longing to be with him, of how much she missed him. Her words must have been welcome relief to a man who was becoming increasingly lonely. Rose was lonely too, as she had been for most of their marriage. Somehow, though, she sensed that her husband was in danger, and her intuition was right. Joseph Kennedy during Hitler's bombing raids on British soil, narrowly escaped death twice.

Rose was determined to keep her children as up to date as possible on the events in Europe, and to that end she awoke early each morning to listen to the radio broadcasts so she could report on the highlights at breakfast. She encouraged her children to understand the issues underlying the conflict. That summer in Hyannis Port Rose took frequent walks alone on the beach, just trying to imagine England under seige. It was Rose's way of staying connected to both the country she loved and her husband. Rose missed England terribly.

Joe returned to America on October 23, 1940, just two years after taking the post as Ambassador. His only souvenir was an air raid siren that eventually hung in the summer house to summon everyone to meals. His departure from Great Britain was accompanied by "GOOD-BYE JOE" headlines in the British newspapers. An editorial in London's *Daily Mirror* warned Joe that England was not dead:

> Mr. Kennedy, U.S. Ambassador to Britain, has pronounced a funeral oration over dead democracy, which he declares is "finished" in England. To say that we are here fighting for freedom is the "bunk stuff." We are fighting for self-preservation. . . . It is for the mass of the people of this country to prove that they and Mr. Joseph Kennedy are wrong.

There was no formal announcement that Joe would be quitting his post. Instead, he just returned to America. President Roosevelt, who had received numerous complaints about his Ambassador and finally decided that enough was enough, summoned Kennedy to his residence in Hyde Park, and asked nothing from him but his resignation. He got it. For Joe it represented the end of everything.

For her part, Rose realized Joe had made an enormous professional error, in believing Britain too weak to be an ally. Rose had a different opinion. She remembered the people she had met, the spirit and strength of the British. They had provided Rose with some of the happiest days of her life, and now, because of Joe, those days would forever be tainted.

Many believed then, and still do, that Joseph Kennedy was an anti-Semite. Rose was always quick to defend her husband against this charge. It is known, however, that the German Ambassador to Great Britain, Herbert Von Dirksen, regarded Kennedy as being sympathetic to the Nazi cause. Kennedy had conversations with the German Ambassador that were dispatched to the Führer, suggesting that Joe and Hitler would get on very well. In one such dispatch, Von Dirksen reported that he and Kennedy had discussed the fact that anti-Semitism existed in America. Von Dirksen assured Hitler that Kennedy understood the German attitude toward the Jews.

Rose was left trying to explain her husband's actions to the world, yet there were many moments when she herself seemed unable to understand them. In later years, either to protect her family from criticism or to soothe her conscience—or possibly to set the record straight—Rose tried to address the charges that her husband was an anti-Semite. She went to great lengths in her memoirs to describe the "Kennedy Plan," a scheme to find homes for millions of Jews who were trapped in Hitler's Germany. But if Joe Kennedy thought these people needed relocating, why didn't he condemn Hitler publicly? It made little sense.

Still, Joe accomplished a few things while he was in England. Aside from succeeding in making his family name a household word in Britain, Joe ran his embassy as smoothly as any Wall Street firm, and he kept the Anglo-American friendship alive, bowing out just before it reached an all-time low.

Back in America, Joe slipped into a deep depression. He could not imagine his future. He figured he had blown it all, and Rose was inclined to agree with him.

Joe wanted revenge against Roosevelt, but his wife managed to dissuade him from this course. She was not however, as successful in alleviating his depression—and she may not have wanted to be. But having gone from heavyweight political figure in London to pariah in the State, Joseph needed support from someone. His daughter Kathleen pleaded with his friends to call and be attentive, and many close to Joe believed he could not live through this humiliation. All he could hope to do now was channel his dreams and ambitions through his sons.

6

The War Years

❧

Just prior to his termination as Ambassador, Joseph Kennedy had launched a Kennedy for President campaign—proof, if there were any doubters left, that he genuinely sought higher office. Now even he realized that that could never be. With renewed fervor, Joe Sr. focused his attention on his two eldest sons, Joe Jr. and Jack.

Joe Jr. was eager to pursue a military career, and his father approved; it was a good move politically. Meanwhile, Jack was making strides at Harvard, penning a senior thesis entitled "Appeasement at Munich," an examination of the situation in Europe leading up to the war. It was later published, retitled, in book form. Boasting an introduction by Henry Luce, *Why England Slept* (the title an intentional contrast to Churchill's *While England Slept*) sold 40,000 copies and even made the best-seller list in America. In Britain the book was even more popular, selling nearly a quarter of a million copies. While the British had disliked Joe, they generally dismissed his antics as the naïveté of a rube who was in over his head. Jack, who was to fight so bravely, helped restore the Kennedy image in England with his commentary on England's slow response to the Nazi threat. Both Rose and Joe had every reason to be very proud of their son. When Joe Jr. became President, his father calculated, Jack could claim a top position in the administration.

Although Rose had mixed emotions about Joe Jr. quitting law school to join the navy, she was too soft-hearted to oppose him. Rose remembered how she had felt as a young girl when her father forbade her to attend Wellesley. She never wanted her own children to have the sort of deep regrets that she harbored. So young Joe went off to serve as a navy flier, believing that he had to do something to help the war effort. Jack soon joined him in the navy, although he had initially been rejected because of the back injury he'd sustained while playing football at Harvard.

Rose worried about her sons. With America on the brink of war, having enlisted was a life-threatening matter. And on August 13, 1944, she learned in the most painful fashion just how life threatening it was. On that summer day, Joseph answered a knock at the door and was greeted by two priests. When he returned, the look on his face transmitted to Rose that the news was devastating. Joseph could hardly bring himself to speak, in fact there was very little to say. His oldest son, the young man on whom he had pinned all his hopes for the future of the family, was dead. It took Joe only a few minutes to break the news, but the horror of the moment would stay with him throughout his life.

Flying a plane loaded with thousands of pounds of explosives, Joe Jr. had been on a top-secret, highly dangerous mission. His plane had exploded in midair over England, and his body was never recovered. Joseph Kennedy never got over the loss of young Joe. After breaking the news to Rose and the other children, he went to his room and locked the door. From that moment on, Joe never mentioned his son's name again. In later years, one insider remembers, he would tell everyone who asked, "Rose can talk of him, I can't."

For Rose, the death of her son meant it was up to her to once again hold the family together. There was little time for her to grieve; instead, she consoled the others. For her own consolation, she turned to God.

The year had already been an emotional roller coaster for Rose and Joe, and more was to come. Just prior to their son's death, their daughter Kathleen, who had moved back to London and fallen in love with British aristocrat Billy Cavendish, the Marquess of Hartington, suddenly announced her intentions to marry. Rose was violently opposed to the match— Cavendish was Protestant. "Kick," as she was nicknamed, was her parents' daughter from tip to toe. From Rose she developed her sense of duty, her ideas about womanhood; from her father she inherited a fierce independence. When she had shared her secret wedding plans with Joe Jr., who'd also been in England, he had given her his brotherly blessing. But Rose had a much harder time accepting Kick's choice and the way she leapt into the match.

All Rose had ever believed in was Catholicism. No other religion, in her view, was truly sincere in its devotion to God and Christ. "We always required the children to maintain their integrity. We are Catholics, of course, and many of the families in Boston were not of our faith. But I tried to impress the children with the importance of observing the commandments of God and of the church." When Kathleen announced that she was going to marry out of the faith, Rose saw her daughter breaking away from the family by breaking with her Catholic roots.

It is still not clear why Rose and Joe were not told that their daughter's wedding would take place on May 6, 1944, or why Kathleen had only a simple civil ceremony at the Chelsea registry office in the center of London. At least Joe Jr. has been there to give his sister away. Now Kathleen had a title herself, the Marchioness of Hartington, but this was of little comfort to Rose, who, heartbroken, heard news of the wedding over the radio. How could Kick have gone ahead with the marriage against her mother's wishes, Rose wondered? She had given so much of her life to her children; how could she be rewarded this way? Yet somewhere in the back of her consciousness Rose must have recalled her own father's resistance to Joseph. When it came right down to it, she couldn't hold a grudge against Kathleen. It took only a month for Kick to return to Hyannis for a visit, where she was welcomed by Rose.

If war made for hasty and intense affairs, it also accelerated the rate of death and tragedy. Within months of their wedding, Kathleen's husband was killed by a sniper's bullet while fighting in France. His death occurred just a few days after her brother Joe's. It is hard to imagine the sorrow in the Kennedy household at that time. Parents grieving a son, siblings mourning a brother, and a young woman faced with widowhood. Everyone looked to Rose for support, and once again she came through.

While the Kennedy family was grieving Joe Jr.'s death, Rose remained alone with an additional burden. Just as her husband could not bring himself to talk about Joe, Rose could never discuss her sorrow about the mental illness of Rosemary. "She could never," one insider says of Rose's anguish, "come to terms with Rosemary's illness. She saw it as a personal failure."

This attitude may have stemmed from a visit to a Boston doctor when Rosemary was a child. The physician had informed Rose that he detected damage on one side of the child's brain, possibly from the forceps at delivery, or perhaps because Rosemary had been dropped when she was an infant. Rose agonized over these possibilities for days. She knew she had never dropped Rosemary, but maybe one of her nurses had.

Above all, Rose blamed herself. If Rosemary had been dropped or had fallen, her mother should have known . . . and she did not.

As the years progressed, Rose saw her little girl struggling with normal, everyday activities. She couldn't pursue sports such as sailing, tennis, and swimming, as her brothers and sisters did. While these problems were troublesome for Rosemary as a young child, they became far more serious as she reached womanhood.

Rosemary was by most accounts the most beautiful of the Kennedy women, and in some respects she appeared perfectly normal. But while her sisters could enjoy the company of young men, Rose worried people would take advantage of Rosemary. She came from a wealthy family and would be a great catch for any opportunist. Indeed, Rosemary loved the attention of men, and Rose feared this might get her into trouble.

Apart from the obvious social concerns, there was also the reality of Rosemary's state of mind. Frequently, the busy family dining-room table, where conversation was always lively, would be thrown into silence as Rosemary flung her food across the room. Temper tantrums were commonplace, and everyone worried about her safety. Then Rosemary's memory began to fail, and it became increasingly difficult to have her at home. As the young woman regressed, Rose found herself tending to what amounted to a baby daughter all over again, without any of the pleasures. Something had to be done. In England, Rosemary had been sent to a Montessori school as a last-ditch attempt to help her adjust. The school, with its different approach to learning, enabled Rosemary to make some progress. But alas, the Kennedys felt it was not enough.

Joe, in customary take-charge fashion, proceeded with his own solution to this problem, knowing his wife would never take action on her own. In 1941, without consulting any other member of the family, Joe authorized a specialist to perform a lobotomy in the hope of altering 23-year-old Rosemary's behavior. The operation left her childlike. Incapable now of staying with the family, Rosemary's options were much reduced. After much deliberation, Joe and Rose decided institutionalizing their daughter was best for all. It was the most difficult decision in which Rose would ever participate. Rosemary was sent to Craig House, an institution for the mentally disturbed on the outskirts of Beacon, New York. Eight years later she was moved to St. Coletta's School in Jefferson, Wisconsin, which has remained her permanent residence. It would be many years before Rose could face her daughter again, and decades before Rosemary returned to the Kennedy compound for a visit. Rose, meanwhile, would live a life of grief and guilt over her first-born daughter. And she would never forgive her husband for submitting their girl to such an irrevocable medical experiment.

Rose grieved over Rosemary's hospitalization in the same way one mourns the dead. In her mind, the beautiful baby Rosemary had been was gone. Just to think of her brought tears to Rose's eyes; she had, she believed, truly lost a daughter. And now she was about to mourn the loss of another.

While Kathleen had disappointed her mother by marrying a Protestant (Joe had not been nearly so opposed to the union as his wife), her parents could not help but extend their hearts to her when she became a widow. So when Kick informed them two years thereafter that she had fallen in love again, they were encouraging. This beau was a married man named Peter Milton, Lord Fitzwilliam—another Protestant, and furthermore not yet divorced from his wife. Nevertheless, Kathleen decided that when he was free she would marry him and asked her father to meet them in Cannes. Joseph Kennedy agreed. Tragically, en route to Cannes to catch a few days' sun before the meeting, Kathleen and Peter were both killed in a plane crash. Their marriage would never be.

Rose's anguish at this sad event can only be imagined. Although she had disagreed with Kathleen frequently over the recent years, her love for this spirited, independent girl must have run very deep. Now there would be no amends, no way to heal the rift that had opened between them.

Part Two

1945–1968:
The Brightest Lights

7

Jack Kennedy and Jacqueline Bouvier

The first half of the 1940s had held very little happiness for Rose Kennedy. She mourned the loss of her first-born, Joe, and her vivacious daughter, Kathleeen, not to mention the tragic canceling out of Rosemary's future. The late '40s and '50s would see it all turn around as the Kennedys at last began their march into national politics. The flagbearer was John Fitzgerald Kennedy.

Joseph Kennedy knew all the strings to pull to get his son elected as a Congressman in the Eleventh District in Boston, and that's where Jack's political career began. During the early years of Jack's quest for power, the family worried constantly about his health. Rose agonized over whether her son would have the physical stamina to sustain any political career (to say nothing of the mental strength he'd need to overcome the public's hostility toward his father). Jack's life had been plagued by illness, which in turn meant that much of Rose's life had been spent losing sleep over him. Joe was also concerned, but he seemed more terrified at the prospect of his second son not making it to Pennsylvania Avenue.

Many people believe that it was Joseph Kennedy who put his son in the White House, but the real power behind the throne was Rose. Had she been born at a different time, there is no telling what heights this brilliant woman could have scaled. After all, she had the ideal background. The daughter of a politician, she knew what to expect of public life. And she understood campaign strategy as only a born politico can.

Stumping for her son was second nature to Rose—it reminded her of the days when she'd stood at her father's side during his campaign swings. Rose, who was then in her sixties, had already achieved celebrity status in Boston. She was now regarded as part of the old school, and when she spoke people listened. Rose was an elegant woman whom people admired, and the newspapers frequently mentioned her public appearances. As one observer at such gatherings pointed out, she had beauty, poise, political savvy, purity, and devotion—difficult qualities to beat. Rose was exemplary.

She was also a remarkably intuitive speaker. She knew instinctively not to force politics down an audience's throat; instead, she constantly played up the fact that she was one of the people, a Bostonian just as they were. A true pro, she researched each group before she spoke so she could tailor her comments accordingly.

~

Most of Boston's voters were women. The combination of the greatly admired, dynamic Rose Kennedy and her dashing, good-looking boy was an irresistible draw to these ladies. At this point, Jack Kennedy was arguably the nation's most eligible bachelor (though he proved too much of a good catch to stay single for very long). In 1946 Jack ran for and won the eleventh congressional seat, where he stayed for six years.

In 1952 Jack decided to run for the U.S. Senate. Rose once again played a pivotal role in her son's success. Boston loved the Kennedys and eagerly turned out for their appearances, especially if matriarch Rose was slated to speak. People were moved by her courage; everyone knew, of course, that she had lost two children. Whenever Rose appeared in public she was immaculately dressed, articulate, and an indefatigable cheerleader for her boy.

There was another, more subtle reason the crowds loved the Kennedys: Because of the family's great wealth, it became something of a status symbol to support them.

Rose was one of the first to recognize the importance of television in reaching voters. When she noticed her son's opponent wearing a tie on TV, she quickly wrote Jack one of her legendary notes sugggesting he try the same attire. Jack listened carefully to his mother's advice, and she rarely steered him wrong.

As it had been for Jack's run for Congress, campaigning for Jack became a family affair, with all the sisters and brothers joining in. When Jack had run for Congress even Honey Fitz campaigned. Sadly, he could not assist in his grandson's later bid for the Senate. Honey Fitz died before the election. His passing on October 2, 1950 was a heavy blow for Rose, but it made her all the more determined to get her son elected.

Rose was almost obsessed with obtaining political power for her family. As far as she was concerned, a vote for Jack was an endorsement of herself as a mother. Every waking moment was spent rallying support for Jack; everywhere she went offered Rose the chance to get one more vote for her son.

On one occasion, when she was taking a cab to Jack's apartment on Beacon Hill, she asked the driver who his vote was going to and was very pleased with his reply: "I think that young fellow Kennedy is going to win." Intrigued by her interest, he inquired further: "You aren't related, by any chance, are you?" "Yes," said Rose, "I'm his mother." "Boy, am I glad to meet you!" said the driver. "Your son owes me one dollar and sixty-five cents." "I'll never do that again," Rose said later.

Rose's hard work paid off. Jack Kennedy beat his opponent, Henry Cabot Lodge Jr., in the Senate race by no fewer than 70,000 votes. Rose's son was on his way to the White House, right on schedule. All he needed was an elegant First Lady to accompany him. That First Lady would appear in the form of Jacqueline Bouvier.

Jacqueline Bouvier was born on July 28, 1929, the event duly noted in the society pages she would one day dominate. Born into a wealthy family, young Jacqueline entered a world that was tumbling into economic disarray. The great stock market crash that would follow three months later devastated the United States. People lost millions of dollars in a matter of days, or even hours.

Although Jacqueline's father, the infamous Black Jack Bouvier, was hurt by the crash, Jackie's childhood was much grander than Rose's had been. At the time of the crash the Bouvier family fortune about equaled that of the Kennedys. Just like Joseph Kennedy, Black Jack wanted to elevate himself socially, and this desire for acceptance was reflected in his every action. Jackie's first home, a luxurious apartment on New York's Park Avenue, showcased her family's wealth.

Jacqueline was a stunning girl, born to beautiful parents. Her mother, Janet, was elegant and perfectionistic, her father movie-star gorgeous. From her earliest years Jackie had wonderful poise and confidence, first displayed publicly in the riding ring. She sensed that she was better off and better looking than most people, and had a strong hunch that she was brighter as well. Her early school days were spent at the exclusive Chapin School in New York, where it become almost instantly apparent that she was an exceptional child. Her grades were superior, and she developed a passion for reading early on. This start in life gave Jackie an air of assuredness that set her apart from most other women. In spite of her strong sense of self, however, Jackie was shy, and that shyness often came across as snobbishness.

Black Jack had plans for his daughter very similar to those Rose Kennedy had for her sons. Jackie, like Rose herself, began making headlines at a young age. At two she was mentioned in the *East Hampton Star* for holding a birthday party attended by some twenty little boys and girls. From this moment on she was rarely out of the news.

One figure in Jackie's childhood would appear years later under bizarre and unfortunate circumstances. Count George de Mohrenschildt was a friend of the Bouvier family who frequently visited them in East Hampton. He befriended the Bouviers in the early 1930s, shortly after his arrival from Russia. To this Russian nobleman the Bouviers were the nearest thing America had to aristocracy, and he particularly enjoyed their large family gatherings on Sundays, when he would join them out in the Hamptons for lunch. Young Jackie was fascinated by this grand-looking man who spoke with a Russian accent and paid more attention to her than did her preoccupied father. As Jackie's cousin Edie Beale recalls, "Jacqueline would sit down on Uncle George's knee—we all called him Uncle George—and listen to his stories." Uncle George became a much-loved member of the Bouvier family. He even wanted to marry into it, first proposing to Jackie's aunt and later to her mother. Both women declined.

De Mohrenschildt resurfaced years later as Lee Harvey Oswald's best friend. The fact that her own Uncle George was a friend of her husband's assassin was a great heartache, not to mention embarrassment, to Jackie. It was a coincidence that would also cause great concern for the Kennedy family. De Mohrenschildt was found murdered on March 29th in 1977 in, of all places, Palm Beach.

To outsiders, Jackie and her sister, Lee, appeared to have a charmed childhood. The reality was different. Jack Bouvier was a heavy drinker, and the effect of an alcoholic father on young Jackie was profound. It broke her heart when, after years of observing her mother and father fighting, she saw her dad pack his bags and leave. Jackie was just 11 at the time, and she idolized her father. After he left she and her sister grew closer, no doubt in self-protection.

The Bouvier household wasn't torn by the type of battling for attention that raged nonstop in the Kennedy home. There were only two children, not nine, so each girl received a generous dose of parental care and guidance. In later years when Jackie found herself surrounded by the Kennedy clan, she often felt the odd woman out—overwhelmed by the constant, frenetic activity and by the sheer number of people.

From the moment Rose set eyes on Jacqueline Bouvier she realized, as did her husband, that this was the woman who could take young Jack to the White House. Jackie epitomised everything Rose wanted to be: elegant, cultured, borderline aristocracy. It would not be fair to say that Rose was jealous of her—Rose had no time for jealousy. But as Rose's secretary, Barbara Gibson, remembers, "Rose was in awe of Jackie; she was intimidated by her." She would have swapped places with Jackie in a second. Rose must have felt particularly stung when Jackie became First Lady, the job Rose had wanted for herself—and might have gotten, had her husband not so badly mishandled his position as Ambassador to Britain.

When Jacqueline Bouvier first met Jack Kennedy, she was photographer and journalist for the *Washington Times-Herald*. For Jackie, it was not love at first sight. She knew Jack had a reputation as a ladies' man, so she was not entirely taken in by his charm. Her father's advice was simple: Play hard to get. It was an effective game, and Jackie was a master at it. Jack, meanwhile, was smitten by the young Bouvier girl. Like his mother, Jackie had made her debut, had studied French, and had a sense of style and elegance that most American women lacked.

In 1953 Jack took a seat in the Senate and made Jackie his date for Eisenhower's inaugural ball. It seems sad even today that, while Jackie had much to offer Jack, he had little apart from his wealth and power to offer her. For most of their life together Jackie would come second either to Jack's family or to his work. Rose tried to help Jackie adjust to her new role. It was like preparing a princess to become Queen, and Rose proved a valuable mentor.

Much has been made of the differences between Rose and Jackie. Their styles were certainly dissimilar, but both women were blessed with astounding reserves of personal fortitude. Each endured the humiliation of husbands who cheated on them. Each put her children's welfare before her own, and each suffered the loss of a child or, in Rose's case, children. On the same day, Jackie and Rose mourned the death of a husband and a son, respectively. For them both, too, Robert Kennedy's assassination was a brutal blow. While at first they may have wrangled over Jack's affections, in the end these two women shared a unique and deeply felt bond.

Bringing a woman of Jackie's background into the family was not a simple assignment. Jackie was a breed apart from the Kennedy clan. As biographer Lester David puts it, "The Kennedy women were clam chowder and Jackie was lobster bisque. She constantly felt like an outsider at family gatherings." Jackie was frequently put off by the clan's aggressive, free-spirited antics. She had grown up in a relatively calm environment, where dinnertime was an elegant pause between other refined pursuits. At Kennedy gatherings dinner often provoked great heated arguments, with all the children grabbing food and screaming. Jackie compared such occasions to dining at the court of Henry VIII.

While Rose tolerated Jackie's often aloof behavior, the other Kennedy women were not so forgiving. Why didn't this woman play touch football like everyone else in the clan? And why was she asking dumb questions like "When I get the ball, which way do I run?" What made Jackie so special? To Rose the answer was simple: Jackie would become First Lady, and because of this she was to be accommodated. Only Teddy's wife Joan would eventually figure out the real Jackie, the woman whom the other Kennedy females called "The

Debutante." Yet the very elements of Jackie's personality that the Kennedy women found puzzling—her aloofness and her ultrarefined demeanor—would captivate the American public and help create the Camelot mystique.

8

A Kennedy in the White House

Rose Kennedy always enjoyed a good wedding, but she had never looked forward to one as much as she did the marriage of her Jack to Jacqueline Bouvier on September 12, 1953. There was something almost magical about these two as a couple. Rose wanted the wedding to feel as bright and stylish and as full of promise as the future she believed lay in store. An official engagement party was held in June 1953 at Hammersmith Farm in Newport. The event got some press coverage, but nothing compared with the miles of newsprint this fashionable couple would occupy.

The wedding of the decade required three months of intensive planning. Rose made a special journey up to Newport to discuss the final arrangements with Jackie's mother, who had remarried the wealthy, well-connected Hugh Auchincloss, but despite both women's determined fine-tuning, the big day did not go by without a hitch.

The Bouviers and Auchinclosses may have possessed more social status than the Kennedys, but on Jackie's wedding day September 12, 1953, as Jacqueline was married at the picturesque St. Mary's Roman Catholic Church in Newport, Rhode Island they demonstrated considerably less class. Jackie had very much hoped to be given away by her father. But the Auchincloss side of the family was footing the bill, and Janet insisted that Jackie's stepfather walk the bride down the aisle. Hugh Auchincloss did in fact give Jackie away, and it upset her a great deal. Her father was even more wounded by the slight. Rose, on the other hand, was not the least bit concerned. Jackie was finally a Kennedy; everything else was moot.

In her later years Rose always spoke of Jackie with great affection. At the time of the wedding she knew full well that marrying into the Kennedy clan was a daunting prospect, and she was sympathetic to the pressures surrounding her new daughter-in-law. Jackie proved herself a wonderful wife from the first, as Rose stated empatically in her memoirs: "I admired the fortitude and courage she showed when Jack had to have his back operations. The first one, when he almost died, was in October 1954, and there she was, still a young bride, deeply in love with her husband and faced with being widowed." Jackie, too, would publicly state her warm regard for Rose. After all, they loved the same man, and both were determined to make him the most powerful figure in the world.

J ack and Jackie's itinerary was firmly set: first the Senate, then the White House. Rose looked forward to the journey immensely.

As she had been in Jack's earlier races, Rose was the driving force behind her son's run for the presidency. She took on the campaign as a full-time job, organizing everything from tea parties to public rallies. At this point in her life Rose had achieved a special status, something akin to that of Britain's Queen Mother. Where Rose Kennedy appeared, people turned up; and when she spoke, people listened. She was a master of political manipulation. In typically astute fashion, she often deferred to her husband so she wouldn't appear too anxious for power. When asked if her son would make it to the White House she would reply, "My husband Joe believes he will win."

But where was Joe Sr.? Because of his dubious behavior while Ambassador to Britain, the elder Kennedy was a distinct liability to his son's campaign. For the last year of the race he stayed in the background, providing funds but otherwise keeping a very low profile. So determined were the Kennedys to keep Joe out of the spotlight that on the night Jack accepted the nomination for President in Los Angeles, Joe was tucked away at an estate eleven miles outside town. When asked about his apparent lack of support for his son,

Joe blamed his age: "Well, I'm 72 and I've had my day; it's the young folks' turn now."

But according to the *New York Times* of January 8, 1961, Joseph Kennedy was considered persona non grata during the last year of the campaign. The paper reported that "it is no secret that the Kennedy campaigners regarded his father as a political embarrassment. Liberals disliked the elder Mr. Kennedy, who had been a friend and supporter of Senator Joseph R. McCarthy. While the son was campaigning as an internationalist during the early years of World War II, the Ambassador to Britain . . . Joseph Kennedy was said to have advised Washington not to aid Britain because Germany would win the war."

Joe's absence during the campaign took its toll on Rose, who was used to her husband's support during these extremely stressful, if invigorating, campaigns. But her son's advisors were right to insist on Joe's invisibility. Not only might he rankle the voters, his presence might make them wonder whether Jack Kennedy or his father would in fact be running the country if Jack were elected.

As soon as the votes were in, Joe immediately ended his sequestration. But though he was in close contact with his son and available for all the important family events—from the birth of John Jr. to Christmas Day photo sessions—it seemed that Joe had indeed relinquished the mantle of power.

While Joe languished on the sidelines, Bobby Kennedy worked ceaselessly to get his brother elected. He mobilized the entire clan, placing Eunice and Ethel in

Texas, Teddy in the western states, and sending Rose, Pat, and Jean out to tour the women's clubs of America. Campaign workers would mumble under their breath, "Little brother is watching you," and Bobby was. He would nag and cajole if he felt a family member wasn't pulling his or her weight, but God help any outsider who criticized a Kennedy. On one occasion, Bobby was questioned about his sisters' campaigning abilities by *Time* correspondent Robert Ajemian. Bobby was about to expound when Ajemian interrupted, suggesting that "Eunice was a little stodgy . . . Pat was a little too flippant." Bobby glared at him and snapped, "If you say anything more I'm leaving the table."

In the end, the efforts of Bobby, Rose, and all the Kennedys—not to mention Jack and Jackie—paid off. Kennedy narrowly beat Richard Nixon in the 1960 presidential race. At last Rose would hear the words she had so often dreamed of hearing: *President Kennedy.* She had honored both her father and her family name. America had its first Catholic President, and with his charisma and brains, it seemed there would be nothing anyone could do to stop him.

The event of the season was the new President's inaugural ball. Rose wore the white chiffon Molyneux gown, embroidered with sequins, that she had donned to meet the King and Queen of England twenty-three years before. It was still fitting attire for a great affair of state—and perhaps even more impressive, Rose still fit into it. Why she did not buy a new dress remains a mystery, but many believe it was a sentimental decision. Meeting Britain's royal family had been one of the most joyful moments in Rose's life; perhaps she wanted to experience that joy again, and had kept the dress in hopes that she would one day have occasion to celebrate another event as grand. Cynics have suggested that this was yet another example of Rose's compulsive penny-pinching, but it's doubtful. Besides, she had proved back when husband Joe had gone off to Hollywood that she could splurge on clothes when she saw fit.

January 20, 1961—the day John Fitzgerald Kennedy would be sworn in as President of the United States—began just like any other for Rose. Waking up early, she marched through the Washington snow to attend Mass at the Holy Trinty Church. When she arrived, however, the church was surrounded by police and media, all there not for her but for her son. It's very likely that Jack's arrival at church that morning gave Rose even more pleasure than his becoming President. Here he was, going to church on his own, without her having to prompt him to do it. Glowing with pride, Rose bent her head and prayed that her son, with God's guidance, would be the leader she had groomed him to be.

A few hours later Rose and Joe Kennedy watched their son give his inaugural address. A mink coat protected Rose from the cold, and her sunglasses prevented the world from seeing the emotion that poured from her eyes. She thought of Joe, of Kick, and of

Rosemary. . . . Would she have forfeited this moment to have them with her today? This is the sort of emotional arithmetic that makes no sense logically, but is familiar to every one of us.

Jack Kennedy approached the podium, dressed in an oxford gray cutaway, a black overcoat, and a black silk top hat. Jackie had chosen a simple Oleg Cassini beige cloth coat with four big buttons and a matching pillbox hat. It was a fashion statement that ignited an era. Jackie's chic, flawlessly tasteful attire become her trademark and inspired an entire industy.

At exactly 12:51 P.M. John F. Kennedy took the oath of office. Rose felt a rush of pride when her son rested his hand on the Fitzgerald family Bible, the very same holy book that had helped her through her darkest moments. She fervently hoped this tome would provide the same strength to her son.

Jack's inaugural address offered hope and suggested immortality:

> We observe today not a victory or a party but a celebration of freedom, symbolizing an end as well as a beginning, signifying renewal as well as change. For I have sworn before you and almighty God the same solemn oath our forebears prescribed nearly a century and three quarters ago. . . . Let the word go forth from this time and place, to friend and foe alike, that the torch has been passed to a new generation of Americans, born in this century, tempered by war, disciplined by a hard and bitter peace, proud of our ancient heritage and unwilling to witness or permit the slow undoing of those human rights to which this nation has been committed and to which we are committed today at home and around the world.

Rose was deeply touched and somewhat surprised at her son's wisdom. His delivery was statesmanlike but resonated with compassion. The future was clear to Rose: JFK would lead a dynasty of Kennedys into the White House. John would run again in 1964 and win, and then it would be Bobby's turn. The family would dominate American politics, because neither Rose nor Joe could imagine anything standing in their way.

Many of the millions listening to Jack speak that day would have agreed with Rose. He concluded with these immortal remarks:

> And so, my fellow Americans, ask not what your country can do for you: Ask what you can do for your country.
>
> My fellow citizens of the world: Ask not what America will do for you, but what together we can do for the freedom of man.
>
> Finally, whether you are citizens of America or citizens of the world, ask of us the same high standards of strength and sacrifice which we ask of you. With a good conscience our only sure reward, with history the final judge of our deeds, let us go forth to lead the land we love, asking His blessing and His help, but knowing that here on earth God's work must truly be our own.

The Kennedy White House was a high-spirited place. As the second youngest President to be inaugurated in the history of America, 43-year-old Jack wanted his administration to reflect the energy that his youth would bring to the capital. He was optimistic and confident—confident enough to appoint his own brother Attorney General. The appointment became something of a family joke. Even before Jack had announced his candidacy, Eunice had remarked, "Bobby we'll make Attorney General so he can throw all the people Dad doesn't like in jail. They'll have to build more jails." Those outside the White House didn't take the action so lightly, suggesting that by appointing Bobby, Jack had virtually placed himself above the law. Lyndon Johnson, Jack's Vice President, reportedly was also concerned about the appointment. But at least one woman totally dismissed the notion that there could be any ethical dilemma inherent in the situation. Rose knew her sons and trusted their integrity.

Having Bobby in the cabinet was part of the Kennedy plan from the beginning, although Bobby himself initially had resisted. Right after the election Jack offered Bobby the position, but he turned it down. He wanted to build his own career as opposed to living in Jack's shadow. And even though Rose wasn't concerned about charges of nepotism, Bobby was very sensitive to them. Jack offered his brother positions in the defense department and even on the White House staff, but Bobby rejected all of them. Jack then proposed to have Bobby appointed to his vacated Senate seat, but Bobby indignantly replied that he would make it to the Senate on his own merits. He told Jack he planned to write for a while and then possibly run for Massachusetts Governor.

By mid-December the only role left unfilled in Jack's cabinet was that of Attorney General. Jack and Joe Sr. were determined Bobby should take the position and set about convincing him. "My father felt that the President should have somebody that was close to him and had been close to him for a long period of time, and he wanted me for the job," Bobby said later. "We had some rather strong arguments out here, all the family—a couple of my sisters; Jack, Teddy, and my father."

One morning Jack lured Bobby to his Georgetown house for breakfast, only hours after Bobby had yet again rejected the Attorney Generalship. Bobby and his friend John Seigenthaler, brought along for moral support, settled down to eat, and Jack started his pitch: "I need someone I can completely and totally and absolutely rely on, somebody who's going to tell me what the best judgment is, my best interest. There's not a member of the cabinet I can trust in that way."

By the end of the meal Bobby had finally relented, but he was uneasy with the decision. Not only was he leery of public reaction to his brother's snatching a prime post for a family member, but he felt his independence diminishing forever.

Bobby may have dreaded being so thoroughly locked into Jack's life, but Rose was ecstatic: "I found myself in the position of being the mother of both the President and the Attorney General, which I found rather overwhelming."

When he came to office, Jack was determined to confront the Soviets in two areas where he felt they had control: space exploration and emerging third-world countries such as Laos, the Congo, and Cuba.

Cuba, he decided, would be his first target. CIA deputy director Richard Bissell had been developing a plan to invade the country, which included the use of 1,500 anti-Castro guerrillas infiltrating the island and then linking up with opponents of the regime. The combined forces would overthrow Castro, eliminating the communist presence that felt so threatening to America at that time. The scheme had been approved by the Eisenhower administration.

The reasons Jack Kennedy became embroiled in the debacle now known as the Bay of Pigs are best addressed by John H. Davis in his book *The Kennedys: Dynasty and Disaster*: "We must once again refer to the Kennedy family ethos of competition, confrontation, and winning. All his life John Kennedy was constantly in competition with someone. . . . His whole personality was geared to confrontation with an adversary. Now his adversaries were leaders of hostile states."

In the first few months of the Kennedy administration the plan to invade Cuba gained momentum. The 1,500 men would be backed by a rebel air force of war-surplus B-26s and escorted to its invasion point by a naval task force. Jack insisted that the military be allowed to review the plans, but he failed to intervene when the CIA gave only verbal briefings instead of providing a written, detailed outline of the operation. He vetoed one landing site at Trinidad Bay because he felt it would take too large a force to complete the invasion, but he did not use the same criterion when Bissell suggested the Bay of Pigs.

On April 17 the first air strikes were launched. But in an attempt to keep the attack low profile, Jack had ordered Bissell to reduce the number of planes from 16 to 6. As a result, only 6 of 55 Cuban planes were destroyed. Despite that, Jack phoned Bissell telling him to continue with the operation as planned: Send in the landing craft carrying the guerrilla army to its destination. Worried about repercussions from the United Nations, Jack then canceled the second air strike, which would have given the invading forces cover. This order basically doomed the invaders—it gave Castro time to counterattack, and Cuban troops pinned the U.S. forces on the beach. Castro's army sank two ships loaded with ammunition, and effectively squelched the invasion.

Twenty-four hours later Soviet Premier Nikita Khrushchev sent Kennedy a message accusing the United States of supporting the military invasion. Khrushchev warned that if aggression toward Cuba continued, the USSR would provide "all necessary assistance" in halting any attack. Kennedy responded with a promise that he intended no intervention in Cuba.

Jack had neglected to tell Bobby anything about the planned invasion until four or five days before it was due to take place. Upon learning of the plan, Bobby was horrified. As it became clear that the mission was crumbling, Bobby supported the suggestion that U.S. troops go in full swing to avoid looking like wimps to the Russians. At one point, with tears in his eyes, he approached Jack, put his hands on his shoulders, and said, "They can't do this to you."

Two days later, Jack Kennedy had to explain the U.S. invasion to the nation and the world. He admitted that he had learned some lessons from the incident, most pointedly that "the forces of communism are not to be underestimated." The full realization had finally hit home: He was one of the most powerful men on earth, and the welfare and security of millions of people lay squarely on his shoulders.

Publicly the President took full responsibility for the disaster, but privately he was devastated and felt he had been let down by his administration and the American public, many of whom felt his actions in Cuba were far too aggressive. And he regretted not consulting with his brother about the plan earlier. He told his friend Lem Billings, "I should have had Bobby involved from the beginning."

"Up until that time," Billings recalled, "Jack more or less dismissed the reasons his father had given for wanting Bobby in the cabinet as more of that tribal Irish thing. But now he realized how right the old man had been. When the crunch came, family members *were* the only ones you could count on. Bobby was the only person he could rely on to be absolutely dedicated. Jack would never have admitted it, but from that moment on the Kennedy presidency became a sort of collaboration between them."

With his new mandate, Bobby's significance increased. He rejected Jack's idea that he take over the

CIA, but became the President's unofficial representative instead. Jack wanted Bobby to be his personal ambassador, moving in the darker circles of power—namely, the intelligence community, which he felt had betrayed him in Cuba. Bobby also was the driving force on a committee formed to conduct an exhaustive postmortem on the Bay of Pigs.

On the home front, the Kennedy administration declared war on organized crime, a move inspired by Bobby, who had made the issue his own since the late '50s. Bobby was fiercely devoted to the cause; he had witnessed ghastly scenes of violence and intimidation when investigating the Brotherhood of Teamsters a few years earlier. The union, he felt, had been deeply infiltrated by the mob. Rank-and-file members suffered beatings, and union funds were embezzled by crooked leaders, particularly Jimmy Hoffa. Bobby was determined to right this great wrong, and he delivered a record number of indictments. His zealous work was admirable, but it made him plenty of enemies within the underworld. Ultimately, it may have cost him his life.

In the middle of December 1961, domestic disaster hit the Kennedys: Joe Sr. suffered a massive stroke. He was near death when Jack and Bobby, along with sister Jean, arrived in Palm Beach on *Air Force One*. The stroke occurred on December 19; five days later Joe developed pneumonia and had to be given oxygen through a tube inserted in his throat. Doctors said he would be profoundly disabled, and they urged the family to discontinue life-support systems. Bobby refused, insisting his father be given every chance to live. Over the next few weeks Joe improved slightly, but he was almost completely paralyzed down his right side, and his speech was greatly impaired. He was able to return home in a few weeks, but from that point on required round-the-clock nursing care.

Rose's initial reaction to Joe's stroke was characteristic: She refused to become alarmed or to believe there was a serious problem. There are some reports of Rose returning to the golf course while the staff and Joe waited for paramedics to arrive, and of Rose refusing to go to the hospital to see her ailing husband until nightfall. By Rose's own account, she followed the ambulance to the hospital and spent most of her time in the chapel there, praying. Rose does concede that when she was first told of Joe's collapse, "none of it registered much on me at the time. After all, everyone feels giddy or weak from time to time. . . . In my own mind, I suppose, I had thought of him just going on and on to some indeterminate time, getting older but meanwhile immune to any serious physical impairments." Joe eventually underwent intensive therapy, the results of which were mixed. After a while he was able to stand and walk a few steps with the help of an aide, but he never regained his speech beyond being able to say yes and no.

For an intensely verbal man like Joe, it must have been sheer hell. Rose put on a brave face and made sure life continued as normally as possible, but she was suffused with sadness for her husband. In the summer of 1962 she wrote in her journal: "Joe's illness. The grief when I see him cry and the pity when I see one who was so strong and independent lie helpless in bed, saying, 'No, no, no.' Sometimes when he means yes." Fortunately, Joe's awareness of the world around him appeared not to have been affected by the stroke, and gradually he adjusted to his condition. He came to family meals, followed the conversations intently, and tried to participate. "Though he couldn't speak," Rose recalled in her autobiography, "he could laugh, and that marvelous grin of his was intact."

After Joe Sr.'s stroke, Jack leaned on Bobby even more, often praising his brother's high moral standards and strict personal ethics. Jack still teased him mercilessly, but Bobby was always the first in and last out of any meeting. No one doubted who the President listened to most closely. As the challenges of the next two years unfolded—the burgeoning civil rights movement, the Cuban missile crisis—Bobby sat at his brother's side, advising on every move. Of the missile crisis, when war with Russia was narrowly averted, Jack said, "This is Bobby's victory. Thank God for Bobby."

Despite the Bay of Pigs fiasco, Kennedy was a popular figure on the international scene, due in no small part to Jacqueline's glamour and his family's charisma. The President was young and handsome, his wife was chic and spoke French, his children were adorable, his mother an icon of strength and piety. Overall, Kennedy and company radiated vitality and sophistication.

Image was everything to the Kennedy administration. To a large extent Rose had inspired Jack's media awareness, beginning with her early comprehension of the role television would play in shaping public opinion. At every turn the President encouraged media coverage of both his administration and his family. His press conferences became legendary; Kennedy's quick wit and effortless charm had reporters practically reeling with delight. But Jack's craving for public attention was not shared by his wife, who treasured her privacy despite the public's fascination with her.

Unlike Jackie, Rose had no desire to skirt the limelight. She assumed the role of first mother with unstoppable energy. There were times when Jackie wanted to remind her mother-in-law that she, not Rose, was First Lady. But she kept quiet, ever mindful of maintaining the Kennedy status quo. Rose relished her visits to Washington and was more than willing to stand in for Jackie whenever she could. She had, after all, earned this position. Her whole life had been dedicated to politics, and now that she was finally in the White House she intended to make the most of it.

Rose gleefully set about contacting heads of states, often to the embarrassment of her son. She'd become an avid collector of books, and she wrote to various authors and world leaders asking them to sign copies of their work for her. Without telling Jack, she sent Soviet leader Nikita Khrushchev a photograph to sign. Concerned that his mother's collecting might spark an international incident, Jack pleaded with her, "If you are going to contact heads of state, please contact me first or the State Department, as it might lead to international complications." Rose was grateful for the advice and jokingly told Jack that she had been just about to contact Castro.

When Rose had visited the McKinley White House as a young woman, she knew she would some day return. Maybe she wasn't the prettiest girl ever to enter the building, but she would make sure that somehow she'd leave her mark on it. As the 1960s barreled ahead, Rose was confident that despite her son's erratic first term, the Kennedys would continue to lead America toward an ever brighter, more prosperous future.

9

A Death in Dallas

∾

The morning of November 22, 1963 was cold and gloomy, but Rose had every reason to be happy. In just a few days the family would gather for their traditional Thanksgiving dinner, and there were birthdays to celebrate too—John Jr.'s on November 25, Caroline's, on November 27. As Rose walked into church at St. Francis Xavier's that morning, she felt especially thankful. By midmorning the fog had lifted, revealing a sparkling fall landscape. The garden around her home was ablaze with black-eyed Susans, marigolds, and chrysanthemums. In fact, so beautiful had this New England day become that Rose and Joe took a ride in their station wagon to absorb some of the scenery.

Rose's son Jack was attending to business as usual this morning. Today his schedule included a trip to

Dallas, where he would speak at an annual meeting of the citizens' council at the Trade Mart. At exactly 11:39 A.M., *Air Force One* landed at Love Field. Ten minutes later a motorcade left the airport for the forty-five-minute ride to downtown Dallas. The President and Jackie sat in the backseat of an open limousine. Seated in front were two Secret Service agents, Roy Kellerman and Bill Geer, and the driver; Governor John B. Connally and his wife, Nellie, took seats behind the driver and in front of the Kennedys. The limo was trailed by a carful of Secret Service agents, followed by another car carrying Vice President Johnson and his wife. A second car of Secret Service agents and vehicles carrying reporters rounded out the procession.

As the motorcade slowly moved through the streets, thousands of Texans stood on the sidewalks and cheered. Around the same time Rose was sitting down for lunch, the limo reached downtown Dallas. After cruising down Main Street, it turned right on Houston and then made a sharp left turn onto Elm Street. As it approached a triple underpass, a sniper aimed a rifle with a telescopic sight from an upper floor of the Texas School Book Depository at 411 Elm. It was exactly 12:30 when shots stuttered across the crowded streets. One bullet struck Rose's son at the base of his neck, a little to the right of his spine. Another hit Governor Connally in his back. A third bullet entered the right rear of Jack Kennedy's head, splattering brain tissue over the car. The President slumped into Jackie's lap as the car suddenly accelerated; a Secret Service agent leaped into the backseat in a desperate effort to shield the President. Many in the terrified crowd dropped to the ground for cover, but a number of witnesses pointed to the Texas School Book Depository as the source of the gunfire.

Three minutes later a Dallas policeman searching the book depository apprehended a man named Lee Harvey Oswald. But when the superintendent of the building identified him as an employee, the officer let him go.

Back in Hyannis Port, Rose was about to settle down for an afternoon nap when a radio playing nearby suddenly blared with the announcement that the President had been shot. According to her recollection of that day, Rose's immediate reaction was mixed. She instantly rejected the possibility that Jack's wound was serious, forcing herself to squelch any panic. Rose had trained herself not to appear too visibly upset at bad news; she considered it her duty to stay strong for everyone else, including her husband, who had taken Joe Jr.'s death so badly. So she quietly returned to her room and paced the floor, praying her son would be alright.

Across America and the world, millions were praying along with Rose. But prayers on this sorrowful occasion were not enough. Rose's anxiety darkened to despair when her son Bobby called and told her Jack's condition was extremely serious. All she could think of now was sparing her husband the terrible news. Within the hour, at exactly 1:00 P.M., President Kennedy was pronounced dead at Parkland Memorial Hospital. Fifteen doctors had tried to save him, but nothing could be done.

While Americans reeled at the news that their President had been assassinated, Rose fought back her shock and grief, focusing instead on her husband. The loss of Joe Jr. had devastated Joseph, and Rose was determined to somehow break this news to him gently. But she needed time to think. By the time Joe awoke from his afternoon nap, Rose had instructed the household staff to tell him that the television sets were broken due to some freakish technological glitch. Radios were inoperable too. Under no circumstances was Joe to be told of Jack's death until the next morning. Rose was a firm believer in giving bad news at the start of the day, so as not to interfere with a good night's sleep.

In the afternoon Rose retreated to the beach. There she paced the shore for hours, trying in vain to come to terms with her loss. Why Jack, and why now? "He had everything to live for," Rose recalled in her autobiography. "A lovely, talented wife, a perfect partner for him, and two beautiful little children whom he adored. He had made such a glorious success of his life and of his presidency, and at last, for the first time since early childhood, he had become really healthy. Everything— the culmination of all his efforts, abilities, dedication to good and to the future—lay boundlessly before him. Everything was gone."

She dealt with her anguish by trying to walk it off, and by praying: *I have to keep moving, walking, pulling away at things, praying to myself while I move and making up my mind I am not going to be defeated by tragedy. Because there are the living still to work for.*

At around four in the afternoon Rose returned to the house; the weather had grown foul and she needed a warmer jacket. She was there to receive Lady Bird Johnson's condolence call, but the new First Lady's words pierced Rose to the heart. "We must all realize how fortunate the country was to have your son as long as it did," Lady Bird told her. Rose did not agree. She had had great plans for John, long-term plans that strectched to the next century. She had envisioned all of it, just as she had with Joe Jr. Mrs. Johnson's words somehow transformed Jack's death, until now a surreal nightmare, into bleak, cold fact. "Thank you, Lady Bird," Rose said quietly. Then she set down the receiver and wept.

As the world learned of her beloved son's death and watched film of Jackie in her blood-stained suit, Rose struggled to comprehend the enormity of what had happened in Dallas. Her nephew, Joey Gargan, had arrived from Boston, and he walked with Rose back to the beach. At one point Joey tried to talk to her about the assassination, but her only response was to advise him to read more, like his Uncle Jack. Her pacing then continued. The two were joined by Teddy and Eunice, who had flown in from Washington. Bobby had remained in the capital to care for Jackie, who was supervising funeral arrangements from there.

Joe Sr. still knew nothing of what had happened, and Rose insisted that be the case until his physician was in attendance on Saturday morning. But although Joe was sick, he had not completely lost his mind, and he soon became frustrated with what he knew to be nonsense. He ordered Teddy to plug in the television set, but Teddy promptly disconnected the other end. He and Rose dared not imagine how the old man would react.

Finally, the next day, Eunice and Teddy broke the awful news. Rose was proud to learn that even as the ghastly information had sunk in, her husband had tried to comfort his children despite his own shattering grief.

Rose took comfort in knowing that Bobby was there at Jackie's side. She knew her son would stand alongside his brother's coffin, and guide Jackie through the whole heartbreaking ordeal. And he, in turn, would have help from his sisters Pat and Jean and from Steve Smith and Sargent Shriver, who stayed in Washington. Teddy and Eunice were Rose's strength at the compound.

As usual, Rose had attended Mass that morning. No one dared approach her. Dressed in black and with her lace mantilla, her grief was so apparent that even the most forthright of journalists could not bring themselves to intrude.

The week that followed was a dismal blur of crowds, reporters, and very public grieving. Every bit of it was broadcast for national and international consumption. The world, and particularly Americans, needed to see their President laid to rest; they were in mourning, too. But for Rose, the exposure made the difficult ritual even harder. She had never sought the sympathy of the public, and surely the millions of eyes watching her every move must have been a tremendous burden even for someone as strong as she.

Then, amid all the funeral arrangements, a bizarre story was unfolding in Dallas—it, too, broadcast over the television. At 7:15 the evening of the assassination, Lee Harvey Oswald, age 24, had been arraigned for the murder of Patrolman J. D. Tippit, who had been shot earlier that fateful day. Later at police headquarters, Oswald was questioned and formally charged with shooting the President. Oswald adamantly denied being the killer. Two days later, television crews scrambled to catch a glimpse of Oswald as he was ushered through a basement corridor for transfer to the Dallas county jail. At 11:20 A.M., 52-year-old Jack Ruby lurched forward from the crowd of reporters and shot Oswald in the stomach. For the second time in thirty-six hours, millions of Americans had witnessed a murder, televised live. Oswald was rushed to Parkland Memorial Hospital, where just days earlier the President had been pronounced dead. At 1:06 P.M., after a frantic attempt to save his life, Oswald died.

The next day, November 25, Rose was told that Ruby had shot her son's alleged assassin. She broke down when she heard the news, but nevertheless was determined to attend the funeral, which would be held in Washington that day. Joseph intended to go, too; he struggled to get dressed, instructing his staff to take him to the airport. But he couldn't complete the journey. Exhausted and spiritually broken, he was taken back to his bed, where he lay beneath the covers watching the burial of his adored son on television.

Rose arrived in the capital to find the family rushing to complete funeral plans. She insisted on making the pilgrimage to the Capitol rotunda, where her son lay in state. Flanked by Teddy and Eunice, she passed the thousands of mourners still waiting to pay their last respects to their beloved President. A hush fell over the crowds as she walked unsteadily toward the flag-draped coffin. She kissed it and left, returning to the White House, where the family was gathered.

That night Rose handed out veils to her daughters and daughters-in-law. She decided not to walk with the others in the funeral procession from the White House to St. Matthew's Cathedral. Nauseated and unwell, Rose battled to maintain her composure, but the tragedy was taking its toll. She arrived at the cathedral by limousine. Despite Cardinal Cushing's intention that she be led immediately to her pew, she held back, insisting she wait for the family. When the coffin arrived she walked shakily to her seat next to Jackie and young Caroline. While the others wept, Rose clutched her rosary, her knuckles white. Having been to Mass earlier in the day, she did not take communion.

The day dragged on. At the burial Rose finally succumbed to her sorrow, subsequently blanking the entire event from her mind. The world witnessed her arrival by car at Arlington as *Air Force One* roared overhead in a ritual fly-past.

With Bobby and her niece Ann at her side, Rose approached the burial plot. For most of the time her eyes were tightly shut while she tried to numb her pain with prayer. The rosary was her lifeline as she stood alongside the cavernous trench that would be her son's final resting place.

At the White House later that day, Rose forced herself to fulfill her duty as the President's mother, graciously accepting condolences from the numerous heads of state and dignitaries who had traveled from around the world to pay their last respects. French President Charles de Gaulle, Emperor Haile Selassie, Irish Premier Eamon De Valera, Prince Philip of England—Rose knew them all and somehow found the strength for brief conversation.

Rose marveled at the dignity with which Jackie conducted herself, smoothly conversing with the visitors despite her obvious grief. Assured that Jackie would be alright, Rose decided she could return that same day to Hyannis Port to be at her husband's side. She had been asked to stay in Washington for young John-John's birthday, but felt that Joe needed her at home.

Bobby remained in Washington to help Jackie. Later Rose learned that the two of them had taken a midnight trip to Arlington Cemetery where they prayed together and left a small bouquet of flowers.

Three days after the funeral Jackie went to Hyannis Port for Thanksgiving and visited her father-in-law in his room, presenting him with the flag that had been draped over Jack's casket. A staff member, not realizing what it was, tucked the flag around the sleeping Joe as if it were a blanket. When the old man awoke he let out a blood-curdling scream, thinking he too had died and was lying in state. Rose went running to her husband's room and was horrified by what she saw. In a very real sense, though, the spirit of Joe Kennedy Sr. did die that week. "He didn't really bother after the assassination," a staff member said. "He sort of gave up. He was never the same."

In the weeks following the funeral, Rose spent long hours in her attic, trying to organize the chaos of memorabilia about her son. She hoped someone would soon ask her for his things to establish a museum. Through the nights she worked like a woman possessed. As the early hours of the morning approached, she'd finally collapse into bed. There she'd anxiously toss, unable to sleep but worried that if she did drift off she'd miss morning Mass. Rose was struggling to keep her sanity, but with the help of God she trusted she would somehow survive.

In early December she and Joe went back to Palm Beach, where they endeavored to provide a "normal" Christmas for those family members able to make the trip to Florida. It was difficult, but with typical Kennedy stoicism they carried on, knowing that this was what Jack would have expected them to do.

A series of memorial services and dedications kept Rose and the others busy throughout the first months of 1964. Industriousness was the best cure for grief, Rose had always believed. She traveled the nation and even visited Paris in March.

Everything about her son's death had been public. Everyone was in on it, but nobody could grasp its enormous effect on Rose. For the sake of her family, she had learned to be the oak that would stand fast no matter what storms came. This time she would have to be strong not just for them, but for a nation.

10

Helping Jackie

∽

During the days and weeks following Jack's death, Rose grappled with the life choices she had made, both for herself and her children. The intense competitiveness, the drive to seek and gain public office were traits the Kennedy children inherited from their parents. Their urge to win was no doubt in their blood, but still, that urge had been nurtured and rewarded by Rose and Joe. The couple pushed, coached, drilled, and, when necessary, harangued their sons to enter the political ring and take no prisoners.

Now Rose's children, her life's work, were being taken from her one by one. Joe Jr.'s death could be attributed to the terrible but necessary cost of protecting democracy. Jack's, however, was a direct result of his being in politics. That first Thanksgiving after the assassination, as she watched Jackie walking along the beach holding little Caroline's hand, Rose ached with misgivings. The two of them looked so lonely. Was the quest for political power worth this misery? A beautiful young woman was widowed, her two small children left fatherless. Rose searched her soul for some formula that would make sense of the choices she had made. But in the midst of her own anguish, she saw one thing clearly: Jackie needed her help. In providing some kind of solace for the grief-stricken young mother, Rose's own spirit would slowly begin to heal.

In the days following the tragedy and throughout the funeral services, Jackie had appeared strong. Rose knew, however, that as soon as the funeral was over and Jackie could escape the cameras, the reality of what had happened would grimly set in. Her life was about to fall apart, and her friends and family were terribly worried. As one insider remembers, "Everyone was concerned about her; she became withdrawn."

When tragedy struck Rose, she knew she could count on her own large family to see her through. But Jackie's family was neither large nor especially close. Rose was determined that Jackie would have the love and support of the entire Kennedy clan to help her survive and recover. Jack's passing acted like a catalyst on the group, pulling them closer, with Rose as the central force.

At first the family members who had gathered at Hyannis Port were doubtful Jackie would want to come to the house for Thanksgiving. In view of all she had been through over the past week, Rose would have understood if she had chosen to stay away. But Jackie wanted to be with Jack's family, and she wanted John Jr. and Caroline there, too. It somehow made her feel closer to her lost husband.

Jackie came away from Hyannis that weekend with a lasting impression of the empathy Rose inspired in her family. There was "something so incredible about their gallantry," Jackie later recalled. "You can be sitting down to dinner with them and so many sad things have happened to each, and—God!—Maybe even some sad thing has happened that day and you can see that each one is aware of the others' suffering." During these difficult days, the Kennedys extended that support to Jackie, Caroline, and John Jr., and their love would sustain that small family.

Few people are aware of just how much Rose helped Jackie during that painful Thanksgiving holiday. The two spent long hours together talking; only Rose and Jackie will ever know the exact content of their conversations. But according to one source, "Rose's courage on that Thanksgiving Day would stay with Jackie forever. Her words would provide the necessary courage for Jackie to continue." When Jackie left Hyannis, she knew she had a mission, a reason to go on living in the wake of disaster. She had a responsibility to face the public and provide some sort of closure for a nation that was still numb with grief. Her first public forum became *Life* magazine.

Within a week of the assassination, Jackie had sat down with journalist Theodore H. White and shared with him some thoughts about her life as First Lady. It was during this interview that the comparison to King Arthur's Camelot first came up.

"When Jack quoted something," Jackie said, "it was usually classical, but I'm so ashamed of myself—all I keep thinking of is this line from a musical comedy." Jackie then quoted the lines from *Camelot*, citing them as favorites of the President:

> *Don't let it be forgot*
> *That once there was a spot*
> *For one brief, shining moment*
> *that was known as Camelot*

"There'll be great Presidents again," Jackie continued, "and the Johnsons are wonderful, they've been wonderful to me—but there'll never be another Camelot again."

So the symbol of the Kennedy era became Camelot, a magic moment in American history when gallant men danced with beautiful women, when great deeds were done, and when the White House became the center of the universe.

Jackie's interview with White touched on a lot of things that were not revealed to the public at the time. Not until a year after her death would the Kennedy Library make public the full transcript of the interview. White had donated the transcripts to the library in 1969 with the stipulation that they not be released until one year after Jackie's death. Those now-published transcripts provide a chilling account of Jackie's experience. Recalling that fateful day in Dallas, still fresh in her mind, she said, "All that ride, I kept bending over him, saying, 'Jack, Jack can you hear me, I love you.' These big Texas interns kept saying, 'Mrs. Kennedy, you come with us.' They wanted to take me away from him. . . . [Kennedy aide] David Powers came running to me at the hospital, crying when he saw me, my legs and hands were covered with his brains . . . From [his forehead down] his head was so beautiful. I'd tried to hold the top of his head down, maybe I could keep it in . . . I knew he was dead." Later Jackie expressed regret at having washed off the blood. "I should have left it there, let them see what they'd done."

The newly published transcripts make it clear that Jackie began planning her retreat from the public eye only days after her husband's demise: "I'm not going to be the Widder Kennedy," she vowed. "When this is over I'm going to crawl into the deepest retirement there is . . . I'm going to live in the place I lived with Jack. I'm going to live in Georgetown. I'm going to live on the Cape. I'm going to be with the Kennedys. Bobby is going to teach Johnny. He's a little boy without a father, he's a boyish little boy, he'll need a man.

"That was the first thing I thought that night— where would I go? I wanted my old house back. But then I thought, How can I go back there to that bedroom? I said to myself, 'You must never forget Jack, but you mustn't be morbid.' I'm going to bring up my son. I want him to grow up to be a good boy. I have no better dream for him. I want John-John to be a fine young man. He's so interested in planes; maybe he'll be an astronaut . . . Caroline—she held my hand like a soldier. She's my helper, she's mine now. But he is going to belong to the men now."

Caroline, said Jackie, had asked her what kind of prayer she should say for her father. "I told her to say either 'Please, God, take care of Daddy' or 'Please, God, be nice to Daddy.' "

Ten days after her husband was laid to rest, Jackie and her two children moved out of the White House. The Johnsons had asked her to stay longer, but there seemed no point. Jackie's love for her children kept her moving forward and prevented her from withdrawing entirely into her sorrow. The knowledge that Rose was enduring similar grief, and that she had also survived the loss of Joe Jr., was a great source of strength to her.

Like Rose, Jackie recoiled from the curiosity of the crowds. She couldn't bear the public's fascination with her and hated the sympathetic eyes of the people who'd gather outside the home of W. Averell Harriman, the former New York Governor and John Kennedy's undersecretary, where Jackie was living temporarily. At the time she had only Rose and the Kennedy and Bouvier families to lean on, along with some trusted close friends. To one of these friends she confided, "The world is pouring terrible adoration at the feet of my children, and I fear for them, for this awful exposure. How can I bring them up normally?" It was at times like these that Jackie would turn to Rose for advice and support, and Rose was always there for her.

Long before the assassination, Rose had felt a certain degree of kinship and sympathy for her daughter-in-law, despite their differences. Rose knew that Jackie had endured a good deal of heartbreak in her life: In addition to coming from a broken home, Jackie had lost a child, a baby boy named Patrick who died just two days after he was born. She had also had great difficulty with the birth of John, who was also premature and had suffered from the same lung infection that would later claim Patrick's life. Rose was aware, too, of the tremendous strain placed on Jackie as First Lady. Rose's willingness to step in and take Jackie's place, playing "first mother," was not just a bid for the limelight. She realized that Jackie was in essence a very private person, and that sometimes she needed a break from the social scene.

Rose was not the only member of the Kennedy family to care for Jackie in the wake of the President's death. Jack's sisters and brothers also offered their help. Bobby in particular considered it his duty to spend as much time with Jackie as possible, and while the more sensational of Kennedy biographers have hinted at the possibility of an intimate relationship between them, those who observed what happened during those painful years dismiss these rumors as cynical and unfounded.

Jackie intended to lead a secluded life now that the world had shifted under her feet. Out of the public eye, she attempted to put November 22, 1963, behind her. *But nearly a year after the assassination,* she was required to relive it all again, testifying before the President's Commission on the Assassination.

Jackie spoke to J. Lee Rankin, the commission's General Counsel, in Washington, D.C. Also present were Robert Kennedy and Chief Justice Earl Warren. An excerpt of Jackie's testimony is reprinted below.

MRS. KENNEDY: We got off the plane. The then Vice President and Mrs. Johnson were there. They gave us flowers. And then the car was waiting, but there was a big crowd there all yelling, with banners and everything. And we went to shake hands with them. It was a very hot day. And you went all along a long line. I tried to stay close to my husband and lots of times you get pushed away, you know people leaning over and pulling your hand. They were very friendly.

And finally, I don't know how we got back to the car. I think Congressman Albert Thomas somehow was helping me. There was lots of confusion.

MR. RANKIN: Then did you get into the car? And you sat on the left side of the car, did you, and your husband on your right?

MRS. KENNEDY: Yes.

MR. RANKIN: And was Mrs. Connally—

MRS. KENNEDY: In front of me.

MR. RANKIN: And Governor Connally to your right in the jump seat?

MRS. KENNEDY: Yes.

MR. RANKIN: And then did you start off on the parade route?

MRS. KENNEDY: Yes.

MR. RANKIN: And were there many people along the route that you waved to?

Rose Fitzgerald Kennedy in the early 1940's.

Rose (at left), her sister Mary Agnes and her brothers Thomas Acton and John Francis with their mother Mary Josephine in Concord, Maine, circa 1897.

Joseph and Rose Kennedy on their wedding day in October, 1914.

Joseph and Rose in Palm Beach in the late forties.

Joseph and Rose (in the white dress) at an Independence Day Party at the American Embassy in London in the late thirties.

Mrs. John Fitzgerald, John Fitzgerald, Rose Fitzgerald Kennedy and Joseph Kennedy at John Fitzgerald's 77th birthday, February, 1940 in Palm Beach.

Rose and Joseph Kennedy and eight of their nine children in Washington D.C. in 1936. From left to right: Teddy, Jean, Bobby, Patricia, Eunice, Kathleen, Rosemary, Jack, Rose and Joseph.

Kathleen, Patricia, Rose, Robert, Jean and Teddy aboard the S.S. Washington in 1938.

*Eunice, Robert, Teddy and Jean on the tennis court,
Palm Beach, Winter 1941.*

*Rose and
Eunice later
that same day.*

above: *Joseph and Rose in Hialeah, FL in 1955.* left: *Joseph and Rose at the Great Lady Ball in the early sixties.* below: *Rose and Joseph.* right: *Rose Kennedy at her son Jack's inaugural ball, 1961.*

Joseph and Rose Kennedy with Jackie Kennedy at the St. Mary's Hospital Ball at Palm Beach's exclusive Everglades Club, March 1954.

President John F. Kennedy and his father, Joseph, the day before Joseph's stroke, December, 1961.

Joseph and Rose out for the evening in Palm Beach in March, 1969.

Rose and the President share a private moment at a formal White House dinner, 1962.

Robert F. Kennedy and his mother, Rose, at Herbert Hoover's funeral, 1964.

Rose and Senator Ted Kennedy share a laugh at her Hyannis Port home in 1973.

Jean Smith and Teddy join Rose in celebrating her ninetieth birthday in 1980.

Teddy and Rose in Hyannis Port next to her cherished photos of Bobby and Jack, 1980.

Teddy and the grandchildren join Rose for a casual dinner in Hyannis Port.

Camera 5/Ken Regan

Ethel Kennedy, Rose, Teddy and various grandchildren listen to one of the kids reading from his favorite book.

Camera 5/Ken Regan

Rose takes a dip in the pool with Eunice Shriver, Teddy and the kids.

Camera 5/Ken Regan

*Rose's last years
were spent alone
in Hyannis Port
at her lovely
home. She was
surrounded by
her beloved family
photos, always
eager for a visit
from family
members.*

Rose waving to her many admirers lining the route of the parade celebrating her ninetieth birthday in 1980.

Rose and a nurse in Hyannis Port in the 80's.

Rose was still taking regular swims in the chilly waters around Hyannis Port until late in her life.

Patricia Lawford, an unidentified nurse and Rose in Hyannis Port, circa 1993.

Teddy was a constant visitor to his mother. Here they share a private moment in Hyannis Port in 1993.

Rosemary's visits to Hyannis Port were seldom but they meant alot to Rose. The last time that Rosemary visited Rose was during the summer of 1994.

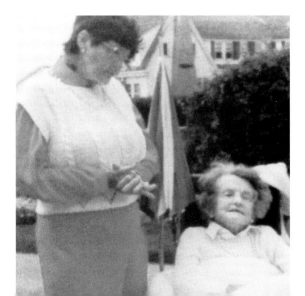

Rose Fitzgerald Kennedy
1890-1995

MRS. KENNEDY: Yes.

MR. RANKIN: Now, do you remember as you turned off the main street onto Houston Street?

MRS. KENNEDY: I don't know the name of the street.

MR. RANKIN: That is one block before you get to the depository building.

MRS. KENNEDY: Well, I remember whenever it was, Mrs. Connally said, "We will soon be there." We could see a tunnel in front of us. Everything was really slow then. And I remember thinking it would be so cool under that tunnel.

MR. RANKIN: And then do you remember as you turned off Houston onto Elm right by the depository building?

MRS. KENNEDY: Well, I don't know the names of the streets, but I suppose right by the depository is what you are talking about?

MR. RANKIN: Yes, that is the street that sort of curves as you go down under the underpass.

MRS. KENNEDY: Yes. Well, that is when she said to President Kennedy, "You certainly can't say that the people of Dallas haven't given you a nice welcome."

MR. RANKIN: What did he say?

MRS. KENNEDY: I think he said—I don't know if I remember it or I have read it, "No, you certainly can't," or something. And you know then the car was very slow and there weren't many people around. And then—do you want me to tell you what happened?

MR. RANKIN: Yes, if you would please.

MRS. KENNEDY: You know, there is always noise in a motorcade and there are always motorcycles beside us, a lot of them backfiring. So I was looking to the left. I guess there was a lot of noise, but it didn't seem like any different noise really, because there is so much noise, motorcycles and things. But then suddenly Governor Connally was yelling, "Oh, no, no, no."

MR. RANKIN: Did he turn toward you?

MRS. KENNEDY: No; I was looking this way, to the left, and I heard these terrible noises. You know. And my husband never made a sound. So I turned to the right. And all I remember is seeing my husband, he had this sort of quizzical look on his face, and his hand was up, it must have been his left hand. And I just turned and looked at him, I could see a piece of his skull and I remember it was flesh colored. I remember thinking he just looked as if he had a slight headache. And I remember just seeing that. No blood or anything.

And then he sort of did this [indicating]. Put his hand to his forehead and fell in my lap.

And then I just remember falling on him and saying, "Oh, no, no, no," I mean, "Oh, my God, they have shot my husband." And, 'I love you Jack.' I remember I was shouting. And just being down in the car with his head in my lap. And it just seemed an eternity.

You know, then, there were pictures later of me climbing out the back. But I don't remember that at all.

MR. RANKIN: Do you remember Mr. Hill [Secret Service agent Clinton J. Hill] coming to try to help on the car?

MRS. KENNEDY: I don't remember anything. I was just down like that. And finally I remember a voice behind me, or something, and then I remember the people in the front seat, or somebody, finally knew something was wrong, and a voice yelling, which must have been Mr. Hill, "Get to the hospital," or maybe it was Mr. Kellerman [Secret Service agent Roy Kellerman] in the front seat. But someone yelling. I was just down and holding him.

MR. RANKIN: Do you have any recollection of whether there were one or more shots?

MRS. KENNEDY: Well there must have been two because the one that made me turn around was Governor Connally yelling. And it used to confuse me because I first remembered there were three and I used to think my husband didn't make any sound when he was shot. And Governor Connally screamed. And then I read the other day that it was the same shot that hit them both. But I used to think if only I had been looking to the right I would have seen the first shot hit him. But I heard Governor Connally yelling and that made me turn around, and as I turned to the right my husband was doing this [indicating with hand on neck]. He was receiving a bullet. And those are the only two I remember. And I read there was a third shot. But I don't know. Just those two.

MR. RANKIN: Do you have any recollection generally of the speed that you were going, not any precise amount?

MRS. KENNEDY: We were really slowing, turning the corner. And there were very few people.

MR. RANKIN: And did you stop at any time after the shots, or proceed about the same way?

MRS. KENNEDY: I don't know because—I don't

think we stopped. But there was such confusion. And I was down in the car and everyone was yelling to get to the hospital and you could hear them on the radio, and then suddenly I remember a sensation of enormous speed, which must have been when we took off.

MR. RANKIN: And then from there you proceeded as rapidly as possible to the hospital, is that right?

MRS. KENNEDY: Yes.

MR. RANKIN: Do you recall anyone saying anything else during the time of the shooting?

MRS. KENNEDY: No, there weren't any words. There was just Governor Connally's. And then I suppose Mrs. Connally was sort of crying and covering her husband, but I don't remember any words.

With that Jacqueline Kennedy had fulfilled her obligation to the commission and to the world. She never spoke publicly of the assassination again.

It was a cold October morning in 1968 when Jean Kennedy Smith called her mother. Jackie had decided it was better if the news about her pending nuptials to Greek shipping tycoon Aristotle Onassis came from Jean. Rose was stunned. Onassis was many years older than Jackie, but more important, he wasn't Catholic. Jacqueline's piety had always impressed Rose; now her daughter-in-law, like Kathleen all those years earlier, was turning her back on the faith.

But the decades had perhaps mellowed Rose. She thought of how much she owed Jackie, the woman who had accompanied her son to the White House, produced two beautiful grandchildren, and shared with her the loss of the man she loved. It took a lot of soul-searching for Rose to accept Jackie's decision, but in the end tolerance won out. Rose pledged to give Jackie all the emotional support she needed, and with a nation temporarily turning against Kennedy's widow because of her engagement to the tycoon, she needed all the support she could get.

Above all, Rose wanted Jackie and her two children to be happy. From the Kennedy family's point of view, Jackie was too young to be a widow, and Caroline and John were far too young to be without a father, or at least a strong father figure. Rose had been acquainted with Onassis for some years and found him rather entertaining. According to Jackie, it was Rose who was the most encouraging of the relationship. Her mother-in-law's approval of the match made it far easier for Jackie to make the transition from Widow Kennedy to Jacqueline Kennedy Onassis.

11

An Apology for the Assassination

The decades since John F. Kennedy's assassination have spawned an entire industry devoted to speculation about who was responsible for the President's death. This book is Rose's story and not a forum for such speculation. But while doing the research for *Iron Rose*, we came across a woman who for thirty years has suffered guilt over what she claims is her part in the assassination. Above all, she wants to apologize to the Kennedy family. Never before has anyone offered the Kennedys such an apology, but former CIA operative Marita Lorenz feels that she can finally speak out now that Rose can no longer be hurt by reminders of Dallas.

Stories about Marita and her life as a CIA operative in Cuba have been featured on the BBC, in the London *Daily Mail*, *Vanity Fair*, and in a book Marita authored for Thunder's Mouth Press. There is no doubt that she was indeed a CIA agent. But Marita, who now lives in hiding, has never before revealed the true extent of her involvement in and knowledge of President Kennedy's assassination.

Here is agent Lorenz's account of what happened on November 22, 1963, how she became part of what she is certain was a plot to kill the President, and how she tried to warn Rose that her son would surely be assassinated. Here, too, are Marita Lorenz's personal letters of apology written years later to Rose Kennedy and her last remaining son, Senator Edward Kennedy.

It was November 24, 1963, and Marita Lorenz sat on the edge of her bed weeping. Thoughts of Rose Kennedy consumed her. Had Rose ever received the letter Marita had mailed to the Kennedy compound in Hyannis Port back in May, warning her that the CIA was out to kill President Kennedy? Why, Marita asked herself, hadn't she delivered the letter in person? Why hadn't she tried to do more?

The top-secret mission to Dallas had felt wrong from the beginning, and Marita knew that if she hadn't bailed out early she would now be responsible for President Kennedy's murder. Sick with grief and remorse, Marita went over and over the events in her life that had led up to this moment. She had been an idealistic young woman just a few short years ago; now she was a tool of the CIA.

Marita Lorenz's career as a government agent had

begun in the late 1950s. Both of her parents worked for the CIA, although Marita will not divulge whether, at the tender age of 19, she had already begun to work along with them. In 1959 her father's ship was docked in Havana harbor; Marita had been traveling with her dad from their home in the States. Perhaps she was intoxicated by the fervor of the Communist revolution in Cuba, or perhaps she was part of an early CIA mission, but in any case she says she soon became lovers with Fidel Castro. Before long she was pregnant with his child. Then, she claims, she was drugged, kidnapped, and returned to the U.S., where she was embraced by national security officials eager to exploit her proximity to Castro. The CIA, she says, took her under its wing and informed her that her next mission would be to assassinate the Cuban dictator. Marita returned to Cuba but aborted the mission. Face to face with the father of her child, she could not bring herself to kill him.

The life of a government agent is lonely and hard, and requires nerves of steel. The assignments are often sinister, and only the toughest can stomach the job. Executions are the most heinous of assignments, and the hit itself is usually only half the problem. The memories of the murder can haunt an assassin forever, occupying waking hours and poisoning sleep. Marita Lorenz never got used to the life; she was tormented by every assignment, but none so much as her mission to Dallas in late November 1963.

Marita Lorenz began to worry about the President's safety in May of that year, after hearing certain agents deride JFK and fantasize about executing him. "They would sit around and joke about killing Kennedy; they would even flip coins," she recalls. Lorenz observed only a few agents behaving this way, and their actions clearly didn't reflect official CIA policy. But she was concerned enough by the statements of some of her co-workers to write Rose Kennedy, pleading with her to convince JFK he could be in grave danger. As far as Marita knows, the letter never reached its destination.

Just months before the assassination in Dallas, Marita claims she and other CIA agents trained with Lee Harvey Oswald. Photographs of these training sessions, she says, were destroyed—possibly by members of the Warren Commission, for whom she later testified. Marita vividly remembers Oswald, and when asked whether he could have been entirely responsible for the President's death, is adamant in her reply: "He wasn't that good a shot, not in the Everglades. And in most hits it's a group of four: two and two. So if you miss, the other [team] is the backup. If it's a big job and you miss, the other [team] gets it, and if it's from a distance nobody whose bullet hits the target ever admits it. But their aim should be the best, and Oswald, I don't know . . ."

On November 20, just two days before the assassination, Marita received orders to go to Dallas. Her traveling companions were several other agents—the same who had joked about killing the President. They carried with them a stockpile of firearms, and the whole scene was familiar to Marita: The group was obviously embarking on a hit. The fact that she hadn't been told exactly how the hit would take place was standard practice; some members of a hit team weren't told the details of a plan until the last instant, when it was too late to back out. With mounting dread, Marita realized that the only important figure who'd be in Dallas when they arrived was John F. Kennedy. Convinced something deadly was going to happen, Marita left the city just twenty-four hours before the President was shot. "If I hadn't left Dallas when I did, I know I would have had the President's blood on my hands," she says.

For all these years Marita Lorenz says she has kept her silence out of respect for Rose, but following the matriarch's death, she felt she had to set the record straight. "I wanted to spare Rose any further pain; she suffered so much as a mother. I have waited over thirty years to tell the complete truth, and now I can. I feel I must say I'm sorry to the family on behalf of America."

Below are transcripts of two letters, one to Rose and another to Senator Edward Kennedy. The letter to the Senator includes a list of unexplained assassinations and the initials of the killers. The CIA community and the Kennedy family, Marita says, will know exactly for whose names the initials stand. The assassins of Jack Kennedy are on the list. Marita says she purposely left out Lee Harvey Oswald's initials because she believes his name is of no consequence.

May 9, 1995

My dear Mrs. Rose Kennedy,
I have always wanted you to know that I've always had the greatest admiration for you.

153

I remember well your spiritual depth, courage, and devotion as the most loving of all mothers, and how very proud you must be.

I am fortunate to have had the opportunity to share with all of America your wonderful family.

To this day, I continue to grieve with you as a mother and share your terrible loss. I would have gladly given up my life to spare your son John's. I am equally sorry that my letter to you from Miami in 1963 never reached you. I will rewrite it and forward it on to your son Teddy.

God Bless You,
Ilona Marita Lorenz

May 11, 1995

Dear Senator Ted Kennedy,

My name is Ilona Marita Lorenz and I have often started, but never completed, writing you this overdue letter. I wrote a prior letter from Miami in the '60s, which I believe was never received.

I wish you to also know that I have always loved, admired, and highly respected our President, J.F.K., your beloved brother, and would have given my life for him anytime.

To this day, I believe that had my letter of warning gotten into the right hands, that terrible event possibly could have been avoided—or at least investigated thoroughly.

My life is all too well documented, and at least now, I want you to know that I am not at all proud to have been a '60s CIA (covert) operative—member of operation 40, operation Mongoose, against Cuba. Instructed and trained by our U.S. military advisers in various techniques of assassination, I had the misfortune of also being in the "inner circles" of this deadly lot of so-called American Patriots, some still active today.

An Apology for the Assassination

∾

It was my *decision* not *to fulfill my assignment (in the name of "national security" also) to terminate the life of Fidel Castro in late '59, early 1960, since I knew him personally.*

Although I had the perfect and only opportunity to do so, I felt then as I do now that such drastic steps would have been ethically, morally wrong, and would not only backfire but is not what our great country should stand for and is no way to handle foreign policy issues.

My associates—all—to this day do not agree, and I have long ago terminated my relationship over the years with them.

I stand by my testimony at the House Assassination Committee (closed executive session hearings, May 1, 1978) but I would have served justice far better had I spoken with you, John's brother.

My documents and writings were altered, marked over, lost, pictures taken by Alexander I. Rorke Jr. "vanished"—as he "vanished"—with my letter to "Camelot" in 1963. I myself almost lost my life due to my testimony, some of which should never be made public.

Today I continue to wonder about the so-called Miami-based patriots—politicians who helped to shape the policy of already three administrations towards Cuba. It should not be overlooked that these once CIA-sponsored Bay of Pigs veterans have much to explain and answer to before they run for the White House . . . And, it should not be swept away lightly that parts they were engaged in—murder, disinformation, deception, violence, and a continuance of other questioned activities.

It was not my intention to write you such a rather depressing letter, but I feel you are the only one who would understand.

I also don't want to sensationalize what was a great tragedy, nor do I want anything, but now that your dear mother has passed on, there should be some closure.

155

Keep up the marvelous work, God bless you and your family,

> *Very Sincerely Yours,*
> *Ilona Marita Lorenz*
> *78/0136*

1—Orlando Letelier—(D.C.)
 V.P.G.N.
2—J.F.K.-F.S.P.D.L.D.V.—(Dallas)
3—Alexander I. Rorke Jr.—(Caribbean) F.S.OB.
4—Jeff Sullivan—(Caribbean) F.S.OB.
5—Camilo Cienfuegos—(Havana 59)
 P.D.L.F.S.M.A.
6—Alice June Lorenz—F.S.F.N.—(N.Y.C.)
7—Irwin C. Karden—(MIA)(BALT.)—F.S.

12
RFK

〜

After Jack Kennedy's death, Rose became increasingly dependent upon her oldest surviving son, Bobby. Transferring her hopes to another son is understandable, but most people would be surprised to know that President Kennedy was only minutes in his grave before Rose started planning Robert's run for the White House. Perhaps focusing on the future was a way of dealing with the tragedy, or perhaps Rose's obsession with political power simply surfaced at an inappropriate time due to her shock. Whatever the reasons for it, people around Rose at the time of the President's funeral characterized her behavior as rather bizarre. Jacqueline Kennedy's cousin, John H. Davis, remembers, "Shaking her hand, I muttered some banality to her about how sorry I was for her and her family, and she surprised me by responding in a cool, utterly controlled voice: 'Oh, thank you, Mr. Davis, but don't worry. Everything will be alright. You'll see. Now it's Bobby's turn.'"

In Bobby, Rose believed she had the perfect candidate. He was a natural leader, taking it upon himself to guide the family through its grief while slowly gearing up to become the second Kennedy in the White House. Above all, Rose admired Bobby's compassion. Of all her children, he had never been afraid to show that he cared.

Robert Francis Kennedy had always been different from his rambunctious brothers and sisters. He was the middle child in a family of nine that included two significantly older brothers and baby Teddy, seven years his junior. Bobby was physically small and often came across as uncoordinated and inarticulate, especially when compared with his adored big brother Joe Jr. or the feisty Jack. His small stature had caused Rose some concern during the early years, but she also believed it helped make him the determined, often stubborn achiever he proved to become.

"He never did become tall," said Rose, "but he became strong, muscular, fast—a fine athlete, in fact, a rather famous varsity football player, an end at Harvard. I think this was the result of raw willpower.

"When he was grown up and in politics, reporters wrote about his toughness and said he was ruthless. I think this is mistaken. He was determined, dedicated, loving, and compassionate. He was a thoughtful and considerate person. He always had the capacity, and the desire, to make difficult decisions. Those who loved him saw this in him, and understood." Bobby's overriding impulse in life was to be like his two big brothers, a difficult task considering that Jack and Joe were eight and ten years older than he. They surely must have appeared to the boy to be veritable gods, but Bobby never stopped trying to meet the standards they set, be it in school, on the athletic fields, or in politics.

When growing up, the first and most obvious arena where Bobby felt compelled to compete was the physical one. While he couldn't match his brothers in strength or speed, Bobby worked diligently at being prompt and independent. He was so intense that even Iron Rose encouraged him to relax a little. Once when he was frustrated that he was taking too long to learn to swim, he threw himself off a boat into Nantucket Sound—he'd either swim or he'd sink. Joe Jr., whom Bobby idolized, leapt in to save him as Jack, who was slightly distant from his kid brother, looked on.

As a young boy Bobby showed plenty of enterprise—and no lack of cunning. One incident in particular stood out in Rose's mind as an example of Bobby's inventiveness. Bobby had announced that he'd taken on a paper route. Rose was quite proud of the lad; she saw the route as "an American symbol of boyhood spunk and ambition." But soon it became apparent that all was not as it seemed. "After a while," recalled Rose, "I found he had talked the chauffeur into driving him. There he was, riding all over Bronxville—making his deliveries from a Rolls-Royce. Needless to say I put a stop to this at once. Shortly afterward something interfered, perhaps he came down with summer flu, and Bobby was out of the newspaper-delivery business."

At age 12 Bobby moved with his family to London when Joe Sr. became Ambassador to Britain. He and Teddy would leave the house every day dressed in gray flannel shorts and maroon blazers. In the morning they'd attend school, and in the afternoons they'd explore the city. It wasn't long before the family realized he was befriending a number of priests at the Brompton Oratory, a training seminary only fifteen minutes from their home. A former altar boy, Bobby had always been Rose's most religious child. Now Bobby learned that the young clergymen, sworn to a vow of poverty, had to buy their own wood. Shortage of money meant shortage of warmth. With facts and figures in hand, Bobby approached his father, making a case for the priests' plight. Impressed with his son's compassion, Joe Sr. arranged a year's free fuel.

The outbreak of World War II and the ceaseless bombing of London forced the family back to the States minus their father. By now a teenager, Bobby enjoyed a few summers of fun in Hyannis Port while his two older brothers fought in the war. These were relatively carefree times for him, but still he was frustrated by his youth and desperate to join his brothers in action. Joe Jr., aware of Bobby's desolation, wrote to him frequently, telling tales of his military adventures. He even invited Bobby for a visit to his base and smuggled him into the copilot's seat of his airplane, letting him take the controls once they were airborne.

In 1944 Bobby, now attending Harvard in his brothers' footsteps, was finally old enough to volunteer for the navy. By the fall of that year he had entered the navy's Officer Candidate School. Rose sent Jack a newspaper article featuring a photo of Bobby pledging his oath. Jack fired off a curt but funny note to his little brother, which Rose kept for decades. It seems that Bobby, as he had often done throughout childhood, had rifled through Jack's closet in search of something suitable to wear for the oath-taking ceremony. Jack wrote, "The sight of you up there was really moving, particularly as a close examination showed that you had my checked London coat on." Jack said he supposed that's what he and all his brothers-in-arms were fighting for—to keep their younger siblings safe and secure. "If you're going to be safe and secure that's fine with me," he continued, "but not in my coat, Brother, not in my coat."

After Joe Jr.'s death in 1944, Bobby became more driven than ever to fight for the cause. Ignoring his father's instructions, he left officers' training camp and finished his military service as a seaman aboard the destroyer *Joseph P. Kennedy Jr.* His only sea duty was a trip to Cuba in early 1946.

Meanwhile, his thoughts began turning to politics. But Bobby felt his father did not have the same faith in him that he had in Jack. A letter he wrote to Joe Sr. at the time plainly reveals Bobby's longing to enter the Kennedy world of politics: "I wish, Dad, that you would write me a letter as you used to Joe and Jack about what you think about different political events and the war, as I'd like to be able to understand what's going on better than I do." After being discharged in the summer of 1946, 20-year-old Bobby offered to work on Jack's first congressional campaign. "It's damn nice of Bobby wanting to help," said brother Jack to a friend, "but I can't see that sober, silent face breaking new vigor into the ranks." Nevertheless, Bobby was assigned to work under Lem Billings, Jack's best friend from childhood, in the East Cambridge section. Jack won, and in the fall Bobby returned to Harvard where he set about reinventing himself.

Said friend Chuck Spalding: "Bobby felt he was weak. He felt he had to toughen himself up and get rid of that vulnerability everyone had remarked on since he was a boy. This was the way for him to get someplace in the family. The drive was incessant, just fierce. He simply remade himself. He got so he could just go through a wall."

This iron will was never more present than during a football game.

Having started the football season in the sixth or seventh squad, Bobby steamed onto the varsity team, and the season ended with Bobby, said to be only a mediocre player, playing with a broken leg for thirty minutes before collapsing.

Rose was astonished: "That, needless for me to say, was over and beyond the courage and fortitude that Joe and I wanted to instill. Even so it had an ultimate and unexpected reward for Bobby. Despite ending his football career the coach allowed him to play in the Yale game to earn his letter—every Harvard player's dream."

After Harvard Bobby attended the University of Virginia Law School, where he received a degree as a result of what one professor called "sheer persistence." His father recognized his struggle. "He is just starting out and has the difficulty of trying to follow two brilliant boys," Joe Sr. said. "This in itself is quite a hardship and he is making a good battle against it." Even the Harvard swimming coach remembered Jack for his floatability while Bobby, he said, struggled through the water. It was an apt metaphor for the brothers' personalities—Jack buoyant; Bobby heavily moral.

When Bobby was just 24 years old, he was already seriously courting Ethel Skakel, a roommate and best friend of his sister Jean. The similarities between Bobby and Ethel's backgrounds were remarkable. Both came from large, active, and wealthy Catholic families. Her father, George Skakel, had started life as an eight-dollar-a-week clerk and went on to create the Great Lakes Carbon Corporation, one of the nation's largest private businesses. Her mother, Ann, was as devout as Rose, attending morning Mass with all of her seven children. The Skakel household was slightly less disciplined than the Kennedys', and Ethel, the sixth child, was renowned for her madcap energy and screaming laughter as she carried out mischievous pranks.

As individuals, Bobby and Ethel were alike in important ways: both had been deeply religious children and both saw the world in terms of black and white, good versus evil. Both Bobby and Ethel were fiercely competitive. But she was certain, where Bobby was slightly faltering; she was lighthearted, where he was moody; she was outgoing, where he was inherently shy. They brought out the best in each other, and Ethel could often be heard urging Bobby to tell a tale or join a conversation.

On June 17, 1950, Bobby married Ethel, becoming the first male Kennedy of his generation to tie the knot. A year later their first child was born, a little girl whom they named Kathleen after his sister. A year later their first boy was born, named after Joe. It was only then that they felt free to name a child Bobby.

In 1951 Bobby went to work for the Department of Justice in the Internal Affairs Division, at the same time committing himself further to the Kennedy family political machine. He was asked by Joe Sr. to be campaign manager for Jack's Senate run against Republican luminary Henry Cabot Lodge Jr. Ever modest and unsure, he responded, "I'll just screw it up." But he relented and headed for Boston, where at last Bobby's light began to shine.

"It was Bobby's first front-and-forward opportunity in the family and he just broke his butt," commented Ted Reardon. His energy came from a selfless determination to make sure Jack won, and campaign workers soon began to refer to pre- and post-"revolution" times. Bobby-the-man was emerging, even if it was for his brother's cause. Joe Sr. provided the funds, but Bobby was becoming the political ramrod, the "heavy," taking on the dirty work and leaving Jack free to be the good guy. He paid a price for the role, soon earning a reputation for being mean, ruthless, abrasive, and short-tempered. The words pained Rose, who knew Bobby to be the most sensitive and caring of her sons. But ultimately the campaign was successful; Jack won the election and took his seat in the Senate, determined to keep his brother close by.

Bobby had other plans; he wanted to carve out his own career. Joe McCarthy was an old pal of Joe Kennedy's, and Bobby landed a post on McCarthy's Subcommittee on Investigations. He had hoped to be appointed Chief Consul but instead was made a subordinate of Roy Cohn's, who was eighteen months his junior and whom Bobby disliked intensely. He worked for the subcommittee on and off for the next six years, growing increasingly dismayed at McCarthy's ideology. Despite arguments, one of which ended with Bobby slamming down the phone saying, "Joe McCarthy, you're a shit," he remained loyal to the family friend. Later Bobby explained, "I liked him and yet at times he was terribly heavy-handed. He was a very complicated character . . . he was sensitive and yet insensitive . . . he would get a guilty feeling and get hurt after he had blasted somebody. He wanted so desperately to be liked."

Some listeners thought Bobby was describing himself.

In 1956 Bobby began his investigation of the Teamsters, which would become a passion and near obsession for him. His father warned him against pursuing the group too intently, worried that Bobby could be putting himself in danger. Bobby ignored him. Joe Sr.

was especially alarmed when Bobby organized a committee expressly designed to expose and indict the Teamsters leadership. His main target was union vice president Jimmy Hoffa, who became his nemesis. After Jack was elected President and Bobby became Attorney General, his battle against the Teamsters intensified. By 1963, Hoffa and his cronies spoke openly about ridding the world of Bobby Kennedy.

In the year before Jack Kennedy took over the Oval Office, only 35 mobsters were indicted. In 1963, 288 were brought to trial. This doubled again within the year. Robert Kennedy's crusade against organized crime was picking up speed, although the elusive Hoffa managed to evade his grasp.

On November 20, 1963—his thirty-eighth birthday—Bobby gave a little speech to friends in the justice department. He outlined the ways in which he had helped his brother with matters such as Hoffa, civil rights, wiretapping, and other administrative issues. It was the last time the Bobby Kennedy of old would be seen. Two days later his world crumbled: The President was shot.

Bobby stayed in Washington to help Jackie manage the funeral. "I thought it would be me," he said, over and over again. Later Lem Billings recalled that "the whole family was like a bunch of shipwreck survivors. I don't think they could have made it at all without Bobby. He seemed to be everywhere. He always had an arm around a friend or family member and was telling them it was okay, that it was time to move ahead."

Stunned and grief-stricken though she was, Rose was aware of how great a loss Jack's death was to Bobby. "Bobby had been very close to Jack, had felt united with him," she said. Now he felt cut adrift, uncertain how to orient himself toward a future alone. "However," said Rose, "automatically and instinctively and very deeply, he wanted to do what Jack would have wanted of him, which in the first urgent priority of things would be to help Jackie and the two children."

Bobby met *Air Force One* when it returned from Dallas on the night of the assassination—carrying Jack in his casket and Jackie in her blood-stained suit. He stayed with Jackie through most of the waking hours of the next few days and went with her to Arlington at midnight after the funeral to pray at his brother's grave and leave flowers there. Bobby was there at Jackie's side until she and the children went to Hyannis Port for Thanksgiving three days after the funeral. Bobby and Ethel chose not to join them. Instead, they and their older children repaired to Florida for a few days to try and regain some perspective on their shattered lives.

Over the next few years Bobby became, according to Rose, a "main pillar of strength in Jackie's life." He acted as "adviser, protector, confidant, and good, cheerful companion whenever he was needed. Ted, of course, did everything he could for her too, but he was younger than she, whereas Bobby was four years older and thus suited by age as well as temperament for the role of protective older brother. She had no really close male kin of her own. Her father was dead. There was a much younger half brother, only a boy. So it was natural and fitting that she should turn to Bobby in this time of sorrow and reconstruction in her life."

But from the moment Bobby placed a tie pin, a silver rosary, and a lock of his own hair in his brother's coffin, he failed to help himself.

He was in perpetual pain. He could not say the words *assassination, death,* or even *Dallas.* He referred only to the "events of November 22." The lights at his Washington home, Hickory Hill, stayed on all night as he struggled in vain to sleep, turning to philosophy in hopes that it could help him make sense of the tragedy. While the others focused on remembering the good times, Bobby was haunted by survivor's guilt. Just as he had when a young man, he started wearing his brother's clothes—a cashmere sweater, an old tweed overcoat he took everywhere with him.

Bobby's friend Ramsey Clark offered this perspective on Bobby's state of mind: "He had been so involved with Jack's destiny that the death was like the death of a self; the prospect of carrying on was terrifying because it was like starting from scratch." The only solution he could see was to continue as keeper of the Kennedy flame. "My brother barely had a chance to get started and there is much to be done," he said.

It became clear during the summer of 1964 that President Johnson was not going to select Bobby as his Vice President, but Bobby wanted to stay in public life and decided to run for the U.S. Senate in the New York State elections. He easily won the Democratic nomination, and Rose and the clan hit the campaign trail for him just as they had done for Jack. Despite a fall in his initial lead, and further negative predictions following his air of uncertainty on stage, Bobby won the election by a substantial number of votes. Teddy, too, was in the Senate, representing the state of Massachusetts.

Bobby did important work while in the Senate, including pushing for aid to groups such as migratory workers and minorities. He brought attention to the plight of poor African-Americans in the South and Native Americans throughout the country. He seemed to go from one oppressed group to the next, trying to gauge what the country's responsibility was to each and to determine how they tied in with his dead brother's legacy. Bobby's attention to the underprivileged provoked the ire of many people who preferred that the voiceless poor in America remain voiceless, and Bobby's office received dozens of threats. There were no bulletproof motorcades for him, and he was often heard to say, "Sooner or later . . ."

While Bobby was crisscrossing the country in an apparent effort to be everyone's savior, his lack of interest in New York State became obvious. His stand on the most volatile issue of the time, Vietnam, was problematic too. While his aides had convinced him to be openly antiwar, his speeches never quite carried the force of his conviction. He came across as confused. But despite all this—and his long-haired, slightly tatty appearance—the public largely loved him.

During his Senate years Bobby became the father figure of the Kennedy clan, which now included twenty-seven grandchildren, ten of whom were his and Ethel's. Lem Billings said, "Bobby was much more openly loving with his children than Joseph Kennedy had been. He touched them all the time. It seems like a small thing, but in the Kennedy family it wasn't. Mr. Kennedy hadn't touched them much when they were young. Jack was the same way—didn't touch and didn't want to be touched."

The presence of his children intensified his longing to make a positive contribution to the nation. One evening as he sat and watched them play happily in the security of Hickory Hill, he said to Lem Billings, "It doesn't seem like much of a world they're going to inherit, does it? I can't help wondering if I'm doing all I should to keep it from going down the drain."

In that spirit, and no doubt compelled by a sense of the inevitable, Bobby decided to run for President in 1968. Joe Sr., although he could not communicate properly, made his displeasure known. Rose had her doubts too, feeling that 43-year-old Bobby, with a houseful of children and demanding Senate duties, had enough responsibilities. There was more than enough time, thought Rose, to run at a later date. But Bobby was adamant, so the troops rallied, and the Kennedys were back on the campaign trail. Rose was 77 but joined the team anyway, providing her famous Kennedy teas and stumping for her son. They may have been slightly divided behind closed doors, but in public they were as united as ever.

"I was almost never on the same platform at the same time with Bob during the 1968 campaign," said Rose.

Still, she monitored his movements like a hawk, noting when he spoke too quickly or let his hair get too long.

During the campaign Rose tried mightily to dispel what she saw as a false perception of Bobby's ruthlessness. "When he was attorney general his probes into labor racketeering and organized crime were marked by his idealism and courage," she said. "He was often threatened with cruel reprisals against his family. I emphasized that above all he was kind. His heart often ruled his intellect. He was open, honorable, and selfless. As his mother I suppose my testimony can be considered biased."

But although the Kennedys were out in full force, the campaign was often listless, and Bobby seemed to lack energy. As one Kennedy worker commented: "Bobby's trouble is that he doesn't have a Bobby." His appearances became feeding frenzies for a public hungry for a touch of the Kennedy magic, but Bobby refused to worry about his personal safety. "If they want to get me they will," he said.

The crucial point in the primary was California, where he was up against Eugene McCarthy, an avid antiwar candidate. Actually, Bobby and McCarthy found little to disagree about, so the race could have proved tricky. On the day of the primary—June 4, 1968—Bobby tried to unwind at film director John Frankenheimer's Malibu house. At noon he went for a swim with his children. Thirteen-year-old David got into trouble when he was caught in an undertow, but his ever-watchful father spotted the helpless boy and swam to his rescue.

With that drama behind him, Bobby returned to campaign headquarters at the Ambassador Hotel in Los Angeles. As the returns came in it became apparent he had won and that McCarthy was out of the race, leaving only Hubert Humphrey as a contender. He said to his old Harvard roommate, Kenny O'Donnell: "Finally I feel that I'm out from under the shadow of my brother. . . . All these years I never really believed it was me that did it, but Jack."

He left his room to make his victory speech and then slipped through the hotel kitchen to meet the press. From nowhere the sound of shots rang out. A bullet pierced the back of Bobby's head, and in seconds the Kennedys' bright young hope lay in a pool of his own blood.

Bobby was rushed to Good Samaritan Hospital, where a few members of his family, including one of his sons, sat at his side. But the injuries were too great, and on June 6, 1968, Robert Francis Kennedy died.

On the night of the California primary, Rose had gone to bed early, thankful that Bobby seemed to be well ahead in the race. She was in Hyannis Port. The next morning she awakened around six, in time for Mass, only to hear on the news that Bobby was being taken to the hospital.

"I really don't remember what I was thinking," said Rose, "except that I was praying, 'Lord Have Mercy,' and thinking, 'Oh Bobby, Bobby, Bobby.'"

Of Robert Francis Kennedy, Averell Harriman said, "He was one of the most gallant men I have ever known . . . If he had been elected President, he would have been a great President. . . . He understood the problems of our time."

Teddy delivered the eulogy at Bobby's funeral at St. Patrick's Cathedral in New York. He summed up his brother with these poignant words: "He was a good, decent man who saw wrong and tried to right it, saw suffering and tried to heal it, saw war and tried to stop it."

In her autobiography, Rose provided her own moving remembrances:

> How sad are our hearts when we realize that we shall never see Bobby again, with his tousled windblown hair, his big affectionate smile, carrying one child piggyback and leading another by the hand—his dog close behind them. What a joy he brought us. What an aching void he has left behind, which nothing in the world can ever fill. We admired him, we loved him, and our lives are indeed bleak without him.
>
> A devoted husband, a beloved son, an adored brother—I know that I shall not look upon his like again.

Part Three

1969–1994:
A Fine Age

13

Chappaquiddick

∽

"He promised me faithfully that he would not run," Rose confided sorrowfully to her godson, Charles Van Rensselaer, in the winter of 1976. The usually stoic Mrs. Kennedy was in tears, shaken and frightened at the thought of Teddy campaigning for the presidency. "I could not stand another tragedy like the deaths of his brothers John and Bobby. I told him I did not want to see him die," she confessed. "I told him that his family needs him too much . . . that John's children need him as a father they no longer have." But despite the promise she'd extracted from her youngest son, Rose knew that ultimately it was Teddy's decision whether or not to run. He had, she knew, his own demons to fight, and he might feel compelled to follow in his brothers' footsteps.

Richard Nixon took the oath of office on January 20,

1969, having ousted Hubert Humphrey in the 1968 election that was to have been Bobby's shining moment. But another election was coming up in '72, and there was one more Kennedy left. Rose wept uncontrollably at the notion of Teddy making the campaign rounds nationwide, vulnerable to hundreds of thousands of strangers who'd want to meet—and if they were lucky, touch—the keeper of the Kennedy flame.

"We've had so many tragedies already," she told Van Rensselaer. "I have prayed to God that Teddy would be led to the right decision. But in the end I have to put it all in God's hands, and I will follow His will. No matter what it is."

Rose's prayers would be answered, but at yet another terrible cost. A young woman's death would forever tarnish the credibility of Senator Edward Kennedy, ruining his chances to hold the nation's highest office. In the end, Teddy would honor the promise he made to his mother not because he wanted to, but because he would have no choice.

It was 1969, and summer had come to Hyannis Port. Rose frequently found herself reflecting on her life. A lesser woman might have been crushed by the events of the '60s, but Rose tried to see it all in light of God's greater plan. She surely had experienced an extraordinary amount of pain, but as she recalled the previous decades, she gratefully thanked the Lord that there had been wonderful times along with the tragic ones. Ever the survivor, she looked to the future. The heartbreak of the past decade, as well as its victories, were fading fast. Perhaps now the hard days were over.

It had taken Joe and Rose a lifetime to build the Kennedy dynasty. It took just one car ride on an empty country road to sink their life's work and their family's reputation. America was already exhausted by the Vietnam War, the Kennedy and Martin Luther King assassinations, and a decade of profound social upheaval. Yet Teddy's journey on Chappaquiddick Island stunned even the most jaded citizens.

The accident at Chappaquiddick is without doubt the most famous automobile crash in American history. So rampant was the speculation surrounding the incident that we may never learn the whole truth. These facts, however, are clear: In the early hours of July 19, 1969, a car driven by Teddy Kennedy plunged off the road and into a Massachussets pond. Inside the car was a passenger, 28-year-old Mary Jo Kopechne, who drowned. Teddy somehow extricated himself and swam to safety, but he waited hours before reporting the horrible event. Later he was charged with leaving the scene of an accident. At the time, many people insisted that he might have been able to save Mary Jo's life. Rose's only son was left trying to explain why he did not. The public outcry lasted for months, but Teddy's conscience would torment him for years.

He was devastated by the accident. The deaths of his four siblings and the sad fate of his sister Rosemary had left him with a walloping case of survivor's guilt, and this latest tragedy only contributed to this burden. As one Kennedy watcher explained, "Ever since Joe Jr.'s death, each one of the Kennedy brothers had a strong sense of survivor's guilt. Then when Teddy was the last one left, his sense of it became even more pro-found. Chappaquiddick made his guilt even worse."

Joseph Kennedy was now a frail old man who had already suffered a stroke. The family agreed that news of the disaster might be too much for him to bear, so they never told him about it. It would be good training for them; in the last years of Rose's life, her children would spare her, too, the more painful family bulletins.

It seemed only Rose could console Teddy after Chappaquiddick. In court he pleaded guilty to the charges he faced and received a two-month suspended sentence. But Teddy remained haunted. Again and again he recounted to Rose the awful details of that night. "No words on my part can possibly express the terrible pain and suffering I feel over this tragic acci-dent," he said publicly. He even contemplated resign-ing from the Senate.

Only Rose fully understood Teddy's pain. She knew how deeply he cared for people, and she realized how seriously he took his mission to uphold the Kennedy name, especially for her sake. Now he felt he had let everyone down. Mother Rose never stopped believing in her son—accepting what he told her about that night on the dark road, and believing that he was a decent, compassionate, and noble man.

The press was not so kind. As the private life of her beloved youngest child now became fair game, criti-cism of the senator from Massachusetts was frequent and often cruel. Throughout it all, Teddy remained a loyal son and devoted, effective public servant. Rose trusted that he would maintain his dignity, help his family, and continue to fight the causes of the people who voted for him. Few in their lifetimes had been through as many emotional firestorms as Teddy, but he always managed to survive because he had the ultimate mentor: Rose. She understood her son, and she learned to forgive him everything.

After the public beating and private hell that was Chappaquiddick, Rose wished fervently that there would be some happiness in store for her beleaguered son. But to her great dismay, she watched as his personal life began to spiral out of control. The first casualty was his marriage.

When she learned that Teddy's marriage was falling apart, Rose was deeply troubled. She knew the stresses facing her son outside of public view: a wife who drank too much, a sick son, his own penchant for women, and the effects of living under the long shadow cast by his dead brothers. She also knew that he had never forgiven himself for Chappaquiddick.

With all her aging might she tried to help the couple, especially Joan. Rose sympathized with Teddy's wife, who had always struggled with the Kennedy way. Life within this legendary political machine could be intimidating and at times brutal, particularly for a woman and a non-Kennedy. Joan bore the burdens all Kennedy wives did: an unfaithful husband and the frustration of playing second to a powerful man, setting aside one's own talents or aspirations.

Yet empathetic as she was, Rose could not allow the

family image to be further tainted. Her sympathy for her daughter-in-law waned as Joan began turning to martinis for comfort and appearing in public looking glassy-eyed and confused. It was not behavior expected of a Kennedy woman. As one insider put it, "There is a rule and Joan broke it, even though she had a disease. What she does in private is her own affair, but the voters must never find out. It was not fitting behavior."

Joan Bennett Kennedy was a woman with a lot going for her—looks, brains, and exceptional musical talent—but like many political wives, she found herself hobbled and eventually crippled by her role as Mrs. Senator. Even women who reach the enviable position of First Lady often find the pressures of the White House too much to bear, despite the privileges.

As the years went by, Joan felt increasingly abandoned. The couple's three children, Kara, Edward Jr., and Patrick, were growing up rapidly, and her husband seemed to enjoy fast cars and alcohol far more than her company. At first she thought it was a passing phase, but after that night when she sat at home three months pregnant and learned that Mary Jo Kopechne had died, Joan felt her happiness slipping away for good. A month later she miscarried for the third time, and she and Teddy decided not to try to have another child.

Rose took to lecturing the couple frequently about the sanctity of marriage and the importance of a politician having a strong, supportive wife standing by her man. Deep down, however, Rose realized her efforts would probably be fruitless. Joan was suffering, and Rose knew exactly how she felt. But while Rose's attempts to free herself by running back to her parents had failed, times were different now; an unhappy wife could in fact break free.

Teddy listened to Rose's speeches but did little to try to change. It simply appeared to him that his marriage was broken and nothing he could do would change the situation.

Other problems also plagued Teddy. All his life he had struggled with his weight, down to being continually teased about it as a child by his lean and healthy siblings. Following Chappaquiddick he gained forty pounds, which he tried to hide with cleverly tailored suits. But he couldn't con Rose. If he dared to ask for seconds in her presence she would scold him as if he were a naughty little boy. Late at night he could be seen creeping into the kitchen, begging eyewitnesses not to let on to his mother that he was sneaking snacks.

His expanding waistline, however, didn't deter the scores of women attracted to Teddy—or perhaps to his position or the Kennedy mystique. Most of his cavorting was carried out in Palm Beach, where as the head of the family after his father's death in 1969 he controlled the goings on and the guest list. Having taken over the Presidential Suite (Jack's former quarters), Teddy was rumored to be entertaining a stream of women there.

Despite reservations and a vague awareness of Teddy's shenanigans, Rose still dared to dream occasionally that Teddy would make it to the White House. As always, Rose was torn between motherly impulses—which had her pleading with Teddy not to run—and the unbridled political ambition she had learned at her father's knee. With a new election coming up, the mother and the politician within Rose waged a fierce battle. It was clearly dangerous for any Kennedy to seek the presidency. But was that more important than one's duty to one's country? America needed Teddy, Rose told herself. America wanted him. Above all, there was the Kennedy name and legacy to consider. A Kennedy belonged in the White House.

Between the mother and the politician in Rose, the politician usually won.

A good many members of the Democratic Party also hoped that Teddy would become President, but his and Joan's behavior made it a difficult hope to sustain. Their marriage was a shambles. Joan, unlike Rose, had led a sheltered and contented life until her baptism of fire into the Kennedy family. Nothing had prepared her for how bold Teddy would be in his pursuit of other women, or for his seemingly insatiable need for new conquests. He didn't bother to hide his affairs, and Joan couldn't force herself to ignore them. Eventually she could not keep her pain private any longer. In 1972 she admitted, "I lost my self-confidence, a very easy thing to do when you suddenly marry into a very famous, bright, intelligent family."

Although her unhappy marriage often plunged Joan into despair, it suddenly took a backseat when she learned that her son had cancer. Just like Rose, Joan and Teddy now faced the hardest battle of all: the serious illness of a child.

It was late 1973 when 12-year-old Teddy Jr. began

to complain of a sore right leg. Tests revealed the child to be suffering from a rare form of bone cancer, chondrosarcoma. The medical decision was to remove his leg. Through this anguish, it seemed no one but Rose could provide the strength to weather the storm. Secretly stunned that God would challenge her family yet again, Rose nonetheless held firm, pacing up and down the corridor outside the operating room muttering to herself, "One must not be defeated, one must not be defeated," followed by, "I must never be vanquished." Every morning and every night she prayed for her family. And always, she was there, the rock of faith and constancy. Whether her prayers were answered or whether Teddy Jr. was simply made of the best of the Kennedy stuff, no one can know. But the cancer was excised, and the boy's spirit was not squelched. On the contrary, Ted Jr. grew up to be a remarkable young man who devotes his life to helping others.

Telling Teddy Jr. that his leg would have to be amputated was, according to the Senator, "the hardest thing I have ever had to do." True to Kennedy form, only half an hour after the operation had begun, Teddy rushed to give his niece Kathleen away at her wedding to David Lee Townsend. He was all smiles for the cameras while inwardly facing one of the worst crises of his life.

After the surgery, young Ted was put through a debilitating course of chemotherapy. Watching their son's constant suffering was nearly unbearable for his parents, who seemed unable to take strength and courage from each other. When the pain became too great, some insiders say that Joan turned again to alcohol. Meanwhile, night after night Teddy would sit next to his boy, chatting to him, reading stories, and showing him movies.

The other two children suffered as well. Patrick was often so sick with asthma attacks that he was prescribed steroids and frequently had to be given oxygen. Fourteen-year-old Kara, enduring the insecurities of most girls her age, was convinced she would catch Teddy's cancer. She acted out her frustrations by experimenting with drugs, running away from home, and fighting with her parents at every possible turn.

With his home life strained to the breaking point, Teddy gave up all thoughts of running for President in 1976. His obligations rested for now with his family, even as he tried staying in the public eye enough to ensure his reelection as Senator. He brought in his nephew Joe to manage the Massachusetts campaign, but the feeling of political unity within the Kennedy family was deteriorating. Rose was unable to take to the road, and many of the next generation were not on hand, too busy in their own worlds of college or work. Some younger Kennedys did work for Teddy's brother-in-law, Sargent Shriver, who had stepped in as a presidential candidate when Teddy stepped down. It seemed to Rose that the time might finally have passed for her to see another son in the White House. But despite the battle scars and the stigma of Chappaquiddick, Teddy was not yet immune to the lure of the Oval Office.

14

Ted Kennedy Comes of Age

As Rose entered her ninth decade, a sea change was taking place in America. Jimmy Carter was President, elected by a population appalled at Watergate and the unsavory exploits of Richard Nixon's inner circle. Carter had sworn that he would never lie to the American public. But after four years of skyrocketing inflation and general uneasiness with his administration, Americans were souring on Carter. Maybe he didn't lie, but he didn't seem to lead very well either. The Democrats were terrified Carter would seek reelection in 1980—a move they rightly figured would end in disaster. As the party searched for a candidate with the charisma to hold the White House for the Democrats, the focus once again shifted to Teddy Kennedy.

Chappaquiddick was still an issue, of course, and the

burning question was, How many Americans would forgive and forget? Oddly, although the accident had appeared to submarine Teddy's political career at the time, it had also given him an excuse to put down the Kennedy torch for a while and concentrate on his work in the Senate.

Whatever may have been happening in Teddy's personal life in the 1970s, he worked passionately in Washington throughout that decade. Senator Kennedy sponsored close to two hundred bills and amendments of his own while working with colleagues on twice that number again. He took stands on vital issues such as handgun control, tax reform, and campaign financing reform, and mounted what became a long-standing campaign for national health insurance. By 1980 Teddy had redeemed himself in the eyes of many of the party faithful.

But could Teddy's good deeds outweigh his trouble-plagued private life? His marriage was now in tatters. Joan was apparently losing her battle with alcoholism. Rose watched, aghast, as Joan showed up for rallies looking puffy and older than her years. No Kennedy wife had ever let herself go this way. Rose couldn't help but remember how hard she had tried always to look fit, healthy, elegant—and this after bearing nine children. Even at age 89 she prided herself on her looks.

Joan's father, Harry Bennett, had once observed that his daughter's marriage to Ted was a "mismatch from the start." Joan maintained that her downfall wasn't the Kennedys' fault: She had allowed herself to be pulled into the clan's lifestyle; she'd lost her bearings and come to judge herself by their standards.

In 1977 Joan had moved out of Washington to live alone in Boston, seeing a therapist three times a week and attending the Leslie Graduate School of Music. Her friend Joan Braden told writer Lester David, "She realized she had to do something about herself and that the only way was to make a physical break with Washington." In Boston, too, she could be shielded from Teddy's rampant womanizing.

Alcoholism is a debilitating, deadening disease. Joan had tried turning to her family for help, but in her view they offered none. "I tried to talk about it," she said in a 1978 magazine interview, "but I was embarrassed by it and Ted was embarrassed by it. Everybody was embarrassed by it, but nobody would really talk about it."

Against this background of domestic turmoil, Ted Kennedy announced on November 6, 1979, that he was officially running for the presidency.

But there was something missing. Joe Sr. was dead, and Rose would never again be strong enough to pull in the cheering crowds on behalf of her son. The mythic Kennedy political machine no longer steamrollered anything in its path; it sputtered along, lurching to avoid scandal and danger. The golden years were in the past.

Teddy himself, usually an impassioned speaker, seemed lackluster. His voice echoed through packed halls, but it failed to touch the minds or hearts of his listeners. Compared with his brothers, as he invariably was, Teddy seemed disorientated and almost insipid. Newspapers reported that his eyes were glazed, his voice strained, and his timing bad.

With brother-in-law Steve Smith at the helm, the family—nephews and nieces included—pulled out the stops. But not only was Teddy traveling in his brothers' slipstream, he was haunted by their violent deaths. He could not risk being shot, so he campaigned under strictest security, driving everywhere in bullet-proof cars. Too nervous to mingle with the crowds, he became insulated from the voters.

The press approached Kennedy with a mixture of morbid fascination and caution. They couldn't resist speculating on the odds of Teddy surviving his campaign. At every whistle-stop an unspoken tension tingled the crowd—would this be the night something terrible happened? At the same time, reporters were wary of the famed Kennedy charm. They didn't want Teddy to seduce them, so they overcompensated with extreme cynicism in their coverage. By the middle of the campaign, news writers were decidedly irreverent, particularly with respect to him and Joan.

Joan had made it clear she would help Teddy's campaign—but under her terms, and her terms alone. She told his aides she would appear only where she wished. For three years she and her husband had been separated, and she had fought to stop drinking and recover her dignity. She wrote her own speeches and became a strong advocate of women's rights.

The press made much of the fact that Teddy and Joan never kissed in public, and when the Senator finally found himself in a position where he could do nothing to avoid a peck on the cheek, the event was broadcast nationwide. Stories about Jack's infidelities and Bobby's alleged affair with Marilyn Monroe were dredged up again. No scandal was left unturned. Gradually, Teddy's bid for the presidency became a tense, joyless ordeal.

Perhaps nothing captured the ugly spirit of that year's campaign better than what happened when 19-year-old Kara visited a church on behalf of her father. Expecting a warm welcome, she instead was confronted by a priest who vociferously attacked Teddy before the entire congregation, prompting the young woman to run crying from the church. Nothing was spared Teddy's kin: In New York one day, Kara was told quite publicly, "You know your father killed a young woman about your age, don't you?"

Finally Teddy faced the inevitable. The dream he wasn't even sure he wanted was not going to become a reality. The night before the New York primary, he summoned the immediate family together to ask their advice. Joe, Bobby Jr., Eunice, and Jean were all that was left of the once indomitable Kennedy machine. Gathered around Teddy in a suite at the New York Hilton, they discussed how they could withdraw from the race and still support Carter for the sake of the Democratic Party.

In the last few weeks of the campaign Teddy looked haggard and pale, despite wins in New York and Connecticut. Polls showed that most of his votes were anti-Carter votes. He finally limped into the convention, and there gave the most rousing speech of his entire campaign. But it was too late.

When asked what he'd learned from the adventure he replied, "Well, I learned to lose, and for a Kennedy that's hard."

In 1982, Teddy and Joan finally admitted marital defeat and got a divorce. Joan received a lump sum of $5 million, plus child-support payments and an annual alimony of $175,000, according to Kennedy biographer Lester David. She and Teddy got joint custody of Patrick, then 14; Kara and Ted Jr. were now young adults living away from home. Joan retained ownership of the Boston house and the Squaw Island home she loved so much, near the compound in Hyannis Port.

Rose was deeply disappointed but certainly not surprised by this final parting of the ways. She had always been very fond of Teddy's wife, and the two women remained close. Rose felt a special bond with Joan for several reasons. There was the empathy she felt for any woman who married into the Kennedy clan, but there was more. Joan had a child with a serious illness, and Rose saw parallels between Joan's heartache over Ted Jr.'s cancer and her own sorrow over Rosemary's mental retardation. Both women knew firsthand that no amount of money helps when you must witness your child's pain. They both had struggled to keep a private tragedy from becoming a public event.

Until Rose's death in 1995, Joan and her children were welcome visitors at Hyannis Port. Joan was the mother of Rose's grandchildren, and in that sense she would always be a Kennedy. She made an effort to be at family gatherings, as long as she wouldn't be crossing paths with Teddy. Joan didn't want to make the situation awkward for Rose or for herself.

Teddy, meanwhile, was spending more of his time at the house in Palm Beach—the mansion Rose had felt elevated her to society's highest peaks. He used it not as campaign headquarters for a powerful political family but as party central, a setting for a string of casual relationships.

By Thanksgiving 1982, family events had become more infrequent, in part because Rose's health was faltering. Frail and birdlike, she sat and picked at her dinner, peering in the direction of whomever was talking. Teddy sat at her side describing what was going on. He wanted his mother to put on a good show for the younger family members.

At the end of a conversation-filled meal, Teddy made a champagne toast to his mother, telling her how they all loved her, how generous she was, and that as always she had provided the best Thanksgiving banquet in Massachusetts. He suggested she might like to speak, and with Teddy's help Rose stood on shaking legs and provided one of her most lucid speeches in many months.

"I want you all to remember that you are not just Kennedys, you are Fitzgeralds too," she said unfalteringly. "The Fitzgeralds are a very famous family in Ireland. There is a public park named for them outside Dublin. The Fitzgeralds came to this country seeking freedom before the Kennedys did. They made money before the Kennedys. When the Irish Catholics had no one to speak for them, the Fitzgeralds did."

In full swing now, Rose spoke fondly of her child-hood, reminding the youngsters that it was important to learn a second language, such as French, just in case there should ever be a time of religious persecution when they would have to pray in a foreign tongue. In a sprightly voice she challenged her family, "Who was the greatest Mayor Boston ever had?"

Bemused but knowing full well the correct answer, Teddy and the clan screamed out, "Honey Fitz!"

Rose described how she had met Joseph Kennedy and had everyone laughing when she asked Teddy whether his father had ever made any money. The family knew they were witnessing something wonderful, and when their matriarch asked who was the prettiest girl in Boston, they were ready with their reply. "You were," they cheered.

"At first I liked Mr. Kennedy, but I didn't love him," Rose confessed to her gathered family. "In time I came to love him very much. Very much."

At this point she seemed to lose her train of thought and looked down at Teddy, saying, "I'm so happy when you're here, dear." She looked fondly at the chil-dren and told them they could visit her whenever they wanted. Then, in a scene so poignant it was almost sur-real, Rose regally walked over to the piano and settled down to play and sing the tunes of her childhood, "Tura-Lura," "My Wild Irish Rose," and finally "Sweet

Adeline." She was perfectly in tune, and she remembered every note.

The next day it was back to business. The question at hand: Should Teddy run for the 1984 presidential nomination? The party faithful wanted him, but Teddy was unsure.

At a lunch attended by his three children, Steve Smith, assorted nieces and nephews, and *Parade* writer Dotson Rader, he put the matter to the vote after lengthy discussion.

Only Rader voted in favor.

"So I guess that settles it," said Steve Smith.

Teddy's political life would be played out within the Senate.

In his private life the divorced Teddy was viewed as a hard-drinking womanizer. This was nothing new. Since the early '70s his exploits had been reported around Washington—and often around the world.

There was the time he went to Paris for Charles de Gaulle's funeral and partied until 5 A.M. the morning of the event, doing the town with an Italian princess. He romanced ski champions and heiresses, actresses and models and society girls of all stripes and ages—as long as they were considerably younger than he. He fondled waitresses, bar-hopped, and generally behaved like a college kid on an all-night binge—only Teddy's binge lasted nearly twenty years. Considering that during this time he managed to hold his Senate seat and remain an active and even trend-setting legislator, one has to marvel at his energy.

Rose kept her opinions about Teddy's social life to herself, but a comment she made to a journalist shortly after Joan and Teddy divorced speaks volumes about her take on the situation. According to Lester David, when the reporter asked her if Teddy was in Virginia, Rose replied, "Virginia . . . I haven't heard of her."

By 1990 Teddy seemed to have calmed himself down a bit. He was still spending a great deal of time in Palm Beach but was partying slightly less than usual. He had been dating the delectable 36-year-old divorcée Dragana DuPont Lickle since the middle of 1988. She and her two children lived in a house facing the Kennedy compound, and the couple were now inseparable.

On Valentine's Day 1991 the couple hosted a spectacular party for friends and relatives, but during the festivities a process server arrived to present Teddy with a subpoena from Dragana's ex-husband, Gary, who was fighting her for custody of the children. The party ended, along with the relationship. Teddy never had to appear in court, but Dragana opted for her children's welfare over the relationship with a Kennedy.

Teddy, now 59, was heartbroken, and he drowned his sorrows in a frenzy of partying. As Cindy Adams mentioned in her *New York Post* column in April 1991, "unsteady Teddy is always ready for beddy," was the rap rattling around Palm Beach—and it was well deserved. He quickly collected a new girlfriend, a 22-year-old college student with whom he was pictured in

St. Tropez. Every night he did the bar circuit in Palm Beach, and during the day he hosted wild yacht parties.

One afternoon he chartered a yacht and invited a group of friends to join him. Teddy and one young woman started kissing and before long were carried away by their passion. According to some reports en route to the cabin and still in full view of other guests, she pulled down his pants and proceeded to please the senator. It was in this frame of mind that Teddy launched the Easter vacation that would add yet another smear to the Kennedy name: the charge of attempted rape.

His friends had long warned Teddy about the effects of heavy drinking on his health. It was not uncommon for him to down a bottle and a half of wine in 15 minutes. Not only was the alcohol dangerous in and of itself, but it was fattening: Teddy was ballooning into a veritable caricature of the bloated politician. And the image was not helped by the disturbing and very public charges of rape brought against his nephew William Kennedy Smith, and the subsequent equally public Palm Beach trial (a scandal that Rose, by then incapacitated by a stroke, would never know). At last Teddy realized he'd better heed his friends' advice and clean up his act. His political career was still going strong, but his sexual escapades were slowly destroying his credibility. In October 1991 he met with his closest advisers—Bobby's oldest son, Joe; his sisters; and Rose—and told them it was time to confront his past.

On October 25, 1991, before a Harvard audience of

800 people gathered to celebrate the 25th anniversary of the John F. Kennedy Institute of Politics, Teddy promised to turn over a new leaf. In this famous mea culpa speech, he said: "I recognize my own shortcomings, the faults in the conduct of my private life, . . . I realize that I alone am responsible for them, and I am the one who must confront them. I believe that each of us as individuals must not only struggle to make a better world, but to make ourselves better too."

One woman more than any other helped Teddy reach this point in his life: Victoria Reggie, a divorced lawyer with two children of her own who was to finally tame wild Teddy.

Teddy was enthralled by the 38-year-old woman, who seemed happily in control of her life. Her father, Edmund, had been a trusted Kennedy aide in the glory days of the late '50s. Victoria remembered vividly first meeting Teddy when she was 10 years old, but he had no recollection of the event.

When they met in June 1991, Teddy was completely bowled over; Victoria, on the other hand, was slightly more cautious. She was familiar with his reputation and had only divorced her husband, Washington lawyer Grier Raclin, in 1990. She had her children, Curran, nine, and Caroline, six, to think about. But throughout the summer the couple gradually spent more and more time together. It was Victoria who coached Teddy in his testimony for the Willie Smith rape trial. When he took the witness stand, it was she who sat in the front row. In the early spring of

1992, Teddy proposed to her, and Victoria willingly accepted.

On March 16, Teddy announced their engagement: "I love Vicki and her children very much. I've known her for a number of years. She has brought enormous happiness into my life. I look forward to our marriage and our life together."

On Friday, July 3, 1992, with thirty family members and friends present, the couple were married. Rose was too ill to attend the ceremony, but afterward Ted, Victoria, and her two children paid her a visit. In the months following, Curran and Caroline would often see Rose in Hyannis Port, bringing her bouquets of flowers they'd picked from the garden or simply keeping her company. Teddy wanted to make sure the youngsters got to know their new grandmother while they still could.

What of Teddy's first wife? Unlike so many Kennedy stories, this one has a happy ending. Joan Kennedy struggled with her alcoholism for many years. More often than not she conquered the bottle, but after the rape trial she drank heavily and was arrested for drunk driving. It was her second arrest in Massachusetts in three years. Her name made the headlines again, and in May 1992, on the orders of a judge, she spent two weeks in an alcohol-treatment center.

It seemed to be the jolt she needed. In November 1992, Joan published a book about classical music for families, entitled *The Joy of Classical Music*. She continued to be involved with A.A., she dated, she regained her great looks, and she appeared in Boston with her head held high. Joan Bennett had found herself at last.

15

Rose on Her Own

〜

After the humiliation of Chappaquiddick, Rose longed for a period of tranquility, uninterrupted by scandal or death. She knew, however, that perhaps her greatest heartbreak lay ahead of her: the death of her husband. Not even six months after the accident, Joe Kennedy died, on November 18, 1969.

The death of Robert a year earlier had signaled the end for Joe. He was already an invalid and had been since his stroke back in 1962. Jack's assassination had taken a huge toll on him, but there was still Bobby to worry about and root for when he decided to run in 1968. The bullet that cut down RFK in Los Angeles effectively sealed Joe Sr.'s demise. His health deteriorated rapidly; he became unable even to feed himself, and as his helplessness increased, so did his depression.

Novembers had been particlarly tough for the clan
ever since Jack's assassination, and this year Bobby's
death was still a fresh sorrow. When Joe suffered another stroke in mid-November, the family gathered
from all over the world to be by his side. Joseph Kennedy had once remarked that "the measure of a man's
success is the kind of family he has raised." By those
standards, not even his enemies could have denied him
a great triumph. Now his children and those of the
next generation came to say farewell to the fiery, indomitable patriarch. Jackie Kennedy, in particular, had
adored her father-in-law. Visits to Hyannis were more
bearable for Jackie because of Joe, and the two of them
had enjoyed and shared endless hours of conversation.

Throughout the last days of Joe's life, Rose remained
devoted. As one insider recalls, "She kneeled by his
bedside, offering prayer after prayer, holding Joe's
hand." And then he was gone. Later Rose would write,
"Next to almighty God, I had loved him—do love
him—with all my heart, all my soul, all my mind."

Considering all the heartache Rose had endured, it
seems strange that those closest to her would at this
juncture worry about her sanity, but they did. "Some
believed Rose would go to pieces when Joe died, that
his death would destroy her," one acquaintance recalled. They were wrong. Instead, Rose frantically
began planning an all-white funeral Mass for her
husband. In the Catholic faith, white vestments symbolize the joy in eternal life, whereas purple robes
symbolize loss.

It was raining on November 20 as the family prepared to bury Joe. The service was private, with only the family and special friends in attendance. About seventy people in all—more than half of them family—sat in the little white church of St. Francis Xavier in Hyannis. It was a surprisingly restrained send-off for a man who had been so much larger than life during his time on earth. The tribute itself—delivered by Cardinal Cushing of Boston, an old friend of the family—was kept short, running only fourteen minutes, but what it lacked in time was made up for in sentiment.

Nine-year-old John Kennedy Jr., who had, despite his youth, become all too familiar with funerals, read the twenty-third psalm with great eloquence. He was joined in the service by several other cousins who served as altar boys and wine bearers. In a voice breaking with emotion, Teddy read a moving and humorous tribute originally written by Bobby: "He called on the best of us, whether it was running a race or catching a football, competing in school . . . 'After you have done the best you can,' he used to say, 'the hell with it.' " Rose closed the ceremony with a prayer: "I thank thee, O my God, with all my heart for all thou has done for me. I thank thee especially for my husband, who with your help made possible so many great joys and such great happiness in my life."

The family then made the eighty-mile drive to Brookline to bury Joe. It would be more than twenty-five years before Rose joined him there.

Rose and Joe had been married for fifty-five years. During that time they had disagreed often, although rarely in public. One subject, in particular, always remained a painful, open wound: their daughter Rosemary. For years Rose had begged Joe to let her bring Rosemary home to visit Hyannis, but he had refused, convinced that such a visit would cause confusion for Rosemary and ultimately lead to heartbreak for Rose. Now Rose, with only herself to listen to, made up her mind to bring her daughter back home.

There were many reasons Rose felt so strongly about Rosemary. The guilt at having (unwittingly or not) allowed Rosemary to be lobotomized no doubt loomed largest, closely followed by guilt at having institutionalized her afterward. But even before her daughter's horrible operation, Rose had tried in vain to come to terms with the girl's retardation. Her first daughter and her most beautiful baby . . . Rose had never worked out in her own mind why the Lord had burdened her daughter this way, and how she, Rose, was meant to handle it.

Over the years there has been much speculation about Rosemary and her exact medical condition. Many articles have been written about her, and while some have been informative—showing the world that even Kennedys can suffer mental disabilities—others have bordered on malicious. Writer Nigel Hamilton has even hinted at sexual abuse, implying that Joe's decision to lobotomize Rosemary was a move to ensure that she'd forget the abuse and keep quiet. Those who had held conversations with Rosemary almost always came to the conclusion that she suffered some sort of word blindness, which led them to wonder later why

Joe had opted for such extreme measures. Yet Rose never challenged her husband's decision.

The Kennedy family has never offered a full explanation for the girl's lobotomy, so the question remains: Was it really necessary for this lively young woman to undergo the surgery and live the rest of her life as an outcast? From our contemporary viewpoint, the answer is a heartfelt no. Yet when Joe made his decision, the technique was brand-new, and he was assured that Rosemary would merely be calmed down, not destroyed. Had he been able to see into the future, who can say what he would have done?

The whole truth about Rosemary's sad fate will probably never be known. The family clearly adored the girl, and there's no doubt she affected them all deeply. Eunice was especially devoted to her, and made her life's work helping those with mental and physical disabilities. Perhaps because of Eunice's kindness, rumor has it that she was Rose's favorite child— although naturally Rose insisted that she loved all her children equally.

Rose's piety had kept her afloat during the many hard times of her life, but where Rosemary was concerned she was terrified. She firmly believed that come Judgment Day she would have no place in heaven if she did not bring Rosemary home. Rose had visited Rosemary at St. Coletta's, the home in Wisconsin where she had lived now for decades, but that wasn't enough. After much deliberation with other family members, Rose decided to bring her cherished daughter back to Hyannis, the place where she had grown up. She hoped Rosemary, now in her 50s, would somehow be able to recall the old days when Joe and Jack were alive, when Kathleen entertained her, and when she was always made to feel part of the fun.

Though Rose had pleaded and planned for this reunion for years, when the moment actually arrived she was beset by apprehension. Would Rosemary remember growing up there? Would she ask questions about why she had to leave, why Rose allowed her to be taken away? Would seeing the house again remind her of the operation—and would she demand to know why Joe had ordered it? Rose was awash in anxiety.

When Rosemary finally appeared, it was instantly obvious that she was an adult on the outside only—mentally, she was still a child. Rose had known this from her Wisconsin visits, but here at Hyannis the condition seemed somehow amplified. Rose was completely bewildered by the situation, and was reluctant to let Rosemary out of her sight for even a moment.

Rose tried to help her daughter by playing piano, having lengthy conversations with her, and generally trying to recapture the old times. Rosemary's moods would swing wildly: Sometimes she'd shy away from Rose, other times she'd throw a full-out tantrum. On many occasions Rose had to fight the urge to run into her bedroom sobbing, as she had when Rosemary was a teenager. Her secretary recalls, "I felt so sorry for Mrs. Kennedy, who simply would not stop trying to make some loving contact with her daughter." It seemed to Gibson that after Joe's death Rose had done a lot of soul-searching about Rosemary's effect on the family. "She said in a letter to Ethel and Bobby's daughter, Courtney, that she felt she had neglected Jack because she was so frustrated and disconcerted by his younger sister Rosemary's insoluble problems."

Rosemary's first visit was hard on Rose—so hard that Joe's insistence that she stay in Wisconsin seemed in retrospect almost understandable. But Rose Kennedy was no stranger to difficulty, and she was willing to suffer Rosemary's disabilities in order to return her to the fold. After her first visit home, Rosemary would become a frequent visitor to both Hyannis and Palm Beach, despite the hardship on her mother. Rosemary made the journey accompanied by nuns, and on every visit Rose would try her best to make her daughter feel at ease and welcome. Eunice, specially trained in dealing with the handicapped, would also pitch in, taking both her mother and her sister on long walks.

On one occasion Eunice attempted to take Rosemary shopping, an excursion that proved disastrous. According to an insider, "Eunice lost her in a department store, and it was picked up by all the newspapers; it was all very embarrassing." There was almost a macabre fascination with Rosemary, no doubt fueled by her family's reluctance to talk publicly about her. Newspapers and magazines constantly ran stories about her, and at least one reporter requested an interview with her at St. Coletta's. A handful of paparazzi frequently hovered nearby, trying to get photos of the poor woman. *The National Enquirer* actually succeeded in getting some shots, which angered the family greatly.

A visit from Rosemary was always a source of both

pleasure and pain for Rose. She looked forward to seeing her daughter, despite the inevitable clashes and scenes. And she was always depressed when Rosemary departed; for days afterward Rose would have severe headaches, feel sick, and sometimes even take to her bed. The suffering her daughter had gone through would torment her mother as long as she lived. But at least now, by having Rosemary visit her often, Rose could live with her conscience and feel as if she were fulfilling her commitment to God.

In other respects old age, even widowhood, was a peaceful time for Rose. Looking around at her beautiful Palm Beach home, she felt quite content. "Life is so beautiful . . . and I am at peace," she told writer Steve Tinney. "I love to walk, it's good for the circulation." Not even arthritis, which caused the 86-year-old to walk with a slight limp, seemed to deter her. "I have been very fortunate with my health and I don't have any problems getting around," she reported.

"You know," she told Tinney, "I love the old house. I have many fond memories of the whole family vacationing down here. But the problem is it's too old and too big just for me." The cream-colored Spanish-style mansion was indeed lovely, but as the years went by Rose spent more and more of her time there alone.

Devotion to God still played a major role in Rose's life. Daily she went to church and prayed, communing not only with God but also with her departed children and husband. As one observer at St. Edward's Church in Palm Beach remembers, "Watching Rose in church you could sense the absolute concentration. She seemed at one through prayer."

After Joe's death Rose found herself daydreaming about the past. So much had happened during the past century; so much had changed since those early days in Boston. As a child Rose had driven the city's narrow streets in a horse and carriage, and now, thanks in part to her son's vision, men had walked on the moon. Despite the rough years and the sometimes cruel disappointments, Rose found satisfaction in knowing that her life had been eventful and she had lived it fully. Rose's old age was marked by a calmness that had much to do with coming to terms with unsolvable problems, such as Rosemary's condition, and accepting the fact that her life was nearing its end.

This isn't to say that Rose sat in her garden all day meditating on the past. Still active socially, she was always a welcome guest in Palm Beach and maintained a healthy schedule both day and night. A typical day for her included a swim, a long walk, and, whenever possible, golf. By night she'd enjoy the odd cocktail reception or charity event. Until the end, her appearance remained of utmost importance to her. She continued to buy designer dresses that flattered her trim figure, paying twice-yearly visits to the showrooms of Givenchy, Dior, Balmain, Grès, Rouff, Ricci, Lanvin, and St. Laurent. Buying wholesale, however, was just fine with Rose. One of her old friends, fashion publicist Eleanor Lambert, paid her this compliment: "Mrs. Kennedy has a much surer clothes sense than Jacqueline Onassis.

She is not a butterfly or compulsive shopper. She knows what she wants; she doesn't go all over the lot. One time she called me from Hyannis Port and asked; 'Where can I get a white raincoat?' She described exactly what she had in mind. I got it from a wholesaler and sent it to her. She was delighted!"

Rose devoted energy to more than just her attire. She was a firm believer in keeping her body in good shape, and she wasn't above buying products that claimed to slow down the aging process. Secretly, Rose Kennedy was vain, and like most women she wanted to stay looking young for as long as possible. One product she couldn't seem to get enough of was a concoction called Wings. Rose had discovered this anti-aging formula in Florida, and according to a former supplier, "She would stop by personally at my home to collect it; staying young was very important to her."

Sustaining the Kennedy family fortune was also a priority. One of the ways this manifested itself was in her compulsion to save money at every turn. Many have accused Rose of being beyond cheap, and in fact she often appeared totally oblivious of the fortune her husband had created. Stories about Rose's apparent stinginess frequently dominated Palm Beach parties, and so lasting was the impression she made that even to this day the matriarch's frugality remains a source of amusement for denizens of the tony resort town.

To the area's store clerks her exploits were legendary. Rose, a regular attendee of the Paris collections, was extremely picky when she chose to buy off the rack. One buyer at Saks Fifth Avenue on Palm Beach's ritzy

Worth Avenue remembers, "Rose Kennedy was always charming, but she would constantly return things after she had changed her mind. If she hadn't have been so nice, she would have been a nuisance." Rose Kennedy, in short, adored a bargain and hated wasting money. She would stop at nothing to save a dollar, while casually dropping three thousand on a designer gown. On one occasion Rose demanded an itemization of an eighteen-dollar candy bill left by her children at a store in Palm Beach—quite an astonishing request for the wife of a multimillionaire and someone who had in one year bought two hundred dresses. But that was Rose's way.

Although Rose was in her 80s and her children well into middle age, not one of them attempted to exchange the parental role with her. Despite each child's considerable achievements, be it Teddy in his role of Senator, or Eunice as founder of the Special Olympics, or Jean Kennedy Smith as Ambassador to Ireland, none of them dared try to guide or influence the indomitable Rose. They would always feel that somehow they were the dependents, she the provider—at least when it came to emotional fortitude.

Eventually, however, even Rose's children had to realize that their mother was getting on in years. Rose's eyes told the story: the beautiful blue eyes that had captivated millions were slowly losing their vision. Although Rose disliked looking old, on a deeper level she had come to terms with her mortality and wanted her children to do the same. For a long while they pushed aside the possibility that anything could actually take their mother from them.

Rose at this point had everything a person could wish for: one of the largest and most productive families in the world, grandchildren who offered great hopes for the future, and her sanity—which in light of what she had lived through was something to be thankful. After Joe died, however, some of those closest to her became concerned that she was spending too much time alone. Perhaps she preferred her own company or believed that in old age she would become an imposition, but in any event Rose got more reclusive as the years went on. She certainly had great training for such solitude; as Joe's wife much of her time had been spent by herself, and she had learned to make her own amusements. Following her husband's death, she had continued in the same fashion.

"Most of Mrs. Kennedy's pleasures came from things she did alone," her secretary reported. "Her daily swim, which had started out as a therapeutic measure, had turned into one of her greatest sources of comfort and well-being. But she preferred to swim alone or with me, because with me she could completely drop her guard. Her newspaper reading was another solitary pleasure. She read several newspapers a day, went through them carefully, and clipped some articles to save."

Rose was by all accounts a fiercely independent woman, but for one who had been so geared toward family, there were aspects of her solitude that worried those around her. One Christmas in particular seemed to suggest that Rose Kennedy was not just alone but downright lonely.

In Palm Beach for the holidays, according to an insider, "Rose had hoped that she would be joined by some family members, and had made preparations accordingly." She had ordered a tree, arranged gifts, and genuinely tried to make a holiday atmosphere. Alas, "no one came, and Rose sat in the house alone. It was very sad, watching this woman on Christmas morning, knowing how many children and grandchildren she had." Whatever the reasons for this atypical Christmas, she never complained or showed any resentment. Considering the devotion of her grandchildren, one can only assume that on the Christmas in question she wanted to be alone.

As much as Rose enjoyed the solitary life in her later years, she always made room for her grandchildren. They visited her, exchanged letters, and as they grew older each came to value her as mentor and role model, the guiding light of their remarkable family.

16
Grandma Rose

∽

Rose Kennedy hated the word *Grandma,* but she was an exceptionally fine one. Her twenty-nine grandchildren were tremendously important to her: They represented the next generation of Kennedys, the bearers of the torch she and Joe had lighted half a century earlier. Although there were occasions when her grandchildren did not live up to Rose's hopes, she loved them all dearly. They in turn cherished their grandma and craved her attention and approval.

Rose took her role as grandmother and matriarch very seriously, but she dreaded being perceived as old. She never forgot the first time someone called her Grandma to her face. Rose was in her 80s, attending an elegant cocktail party and feeling as alluring as she had in her prime. Then her son-in-law, Sargent

Shriver, caught sight of her for the first time that evening, and shouted a happy "Grandma!" in greeting.
Rose Kennedy felt instantly deglamorized. Yet despite
other moments when her vanity temporarily eclipsed
her familial pride, Rose proved herself to be a natural
at the art of grandmothering. And over the years she
even became used to the name Grandma Rose.

Those who admire Rose Kennedy's efforts to nur-
ture and guide more than two dozen grandchildren
might be surprised to learn that she herself lacked a
strong grandmother figure. Rose's paternal grandmother, Rose Mary Fitzgerald, died before she was
born, and her maternal grandmother, Josie Hannon
(fleetingly referred to by Rose in her autobiography
merely in terms of living in a hilltop house in Acton,
Massachusetts) did not play a vital part in her formative
years. Nevertheless, Rose become as strong and influ-
ential a grandmother as she had been a parent.

True to form, Rose approached grandmothering
with a sense of duty as well as pleasure. Grandchildren
were not to be spoiled; rather, they were to be taught.
Old fashioned and often didactic, she employed the
same techniques with them as she had to shape the
characters of her own children. The formula was often
repeated in the dozens of letters she penned to the
grandchildren, instructing them to drink milk, attend
church, and live good, decent Christian lives.

Not surprisingly, Rose's primary concern was raising
another generation of devout Catholics. Ted Kennedy's
friend Claude Hooton pointed out, "There is an immense amount of faith in that family, and it comes

from Rose. Rose once told me that I should live every day as if it were the last—not in the sense that I should blast off and have a helluva time. It was in the sense that I should be a pretty good guy."

Famous within the family for quoting the Bible and other religious teachings to her grandchildren, Rose was especially fond of Cardinal Newman's renowned passage: "God has created me to do Him some definite service. He has committed some work to me which He has not committed to another. I have my mission—I may never know it in this life, but I shall be told it in the next. I am a link in a chain, a bond of connection between persons. He has not created me for naught. I shall do good, I shall do His work."

In her campaign to encourage their spiritual side, Rose made sure each grandchild was presented with a rosary. She suggested suitable Christian television programs for them to watch and urged their parents to subscribe to Christian magazines. Yet as her grandchildren grew older, Rose became sadly aware that a number of them were not particularly pious. Though she may have been disappointed, Rose didn't let this hinder her relationships with the young people. Instead she carefully avoided arguments about faith or commitment to the Catholic Church.

Rose expected far more from her grandchildren than religious devotion, however. She gave them the best gift a grandmother or any adult can give a child: respect. Even when they were infants, she eschewed baby talk. Rose never patronized the grandchildren, assuming that each little Kennedy would be bright, witty, talented, and humble—and treating them as if they were. From the time they uttered their first words, Rose included the youngsters in the mealtime quizzes she and Joe had perfected on their own brood. Her questions covered geography and history, religion and current affairs. Fortunately for the grandkids, Rose's approach was considerably lighter than Joe's had been. She loved to play word games with them; these had been Jack's favorite, and playing them always brought Rose a few pleasant memories.

A love of politics still coursed through Rose's veins, as it would until her death. Those who knew her well claim she secretly longed for her grandchildren to uphold the family tradition and go into public service. Every Kennedy grandchild received from Grandma Rose a copy of the Declaration of Independence and one of Longfellow's famous poems, "Paul Revere's Ride."

Rose's first grandchild was a girl. Kathleen Harington Kennedy was born on July 4, 1951 to Robert and Ethel Kennedy. Being the first guaranteed her a special place in Rose's heart, and Kathleen in turn always had great affection for her grandmother. Perhaps because the two were so close, Kathleen was never afraid to debate Rose on an assortment of topics.

"She and I do not agree about some things that I consider important," Kathleen has admitted. "But that's alright, I defend her right to disagree. She's had an impressively full life, and is to be admired for it.

We've had major differences—still do. But I'd say now that she's wonderful and fantastic."

Despite her unspecified differences with her grandmother, Kathleen nevertheless attended a Catholic school (Sacred Heart Country Day School in Bethesda, Maryland) and named the third of her children Rose. Kathleen was the first recipient of Rose's legendary missives. Reading those letters over forty years later, they still ring with compassion and humor. Although they were composed on the formal letterhead of Mrs. Joseph P. Kennedy, their content is consistently warm, encouraging, and instructive. In one of the earliest, Rose expresses her sorrow that Kathleen doesn't live close enough to her, confiding that she wishes they could have lunch together more often and that she could read Kathleen a bedtime story every night.

Rose and Kathleen shared a love of the ballet, and Rose took her to see *The Nutcracker* when the girl was only eight or nine years old. Naturally, Rose stressed the great importance of education, encouraging Kathleen to study hard. A knowledge of history was crucial, Rose taught the young girl, especially given the fact that the Kennedys recently played a large part in it.

More than a teacher, Rose tried hard to be a friend to her grandchildren. She gamely struggled to understand the styles and mores of the often bewildering younger generation, whose ways were so totally foreign to her. Kathleen now recounts taking a bicycle tour through France with a friend named Ann and surprising Rose in Paris, where she was staying at the luxurious Plaza Athénée. Rose had no idea Kathleen was in Paris and was completely unprepared for her arrival. On being greeted in the elegant lobby of the fine hotel by two scruffy teenagers in jeans carrying backpacks, Rose was initially taken aback.

It didn't take long, however, for her to swing into action. She quickly sent the two girls up to her room, where they both took well-needed baths. Although she insisted they stay at the hotel as her guests, Kathleen and Ann felt out of place amid all the opulence and instead found a cheap hotel on the Left Bank. A concerned Rose asked the Plaza Athénée desk clerk if the hotel was safe, and when the clerk couldn't reassure her, she hailed a taxi and took the girls there herself.

Kathleen recalls, "She took us over and, with her long Dior gown on, walked into this halfway shabby hotel and interviewed the concierge there. 'Will these girls be safe? Is there a shower?' . . . But she was terrific about it, and she kept her sense of humor throughout."

Over the next few days, Rose spent time with Kathleen and Ann sightseeing in Paris. In the process, she quizzed Kathleen about architecture, offered to buy her a Dior gown, and on the whole treated her like the cherished friend she was.

Kathleen offered another insight into life with her grandparents in a book by photographer Frank Teti, *Kennedy: The New Generation*.

> For all of us cousins, Hyannis Port was dominated by "the big house" and its inhabitants, Grandma and Grandpa. They set the rules. "No dogs" was a particularly burdensome regulation for our family, who for many years owned and loved a St. Bernard, an Irish setter, an Old English

sheep dog, and a black retriever. Each August, and often the last two weeks of July, they were banished to Washington. However, a few years ago my mother, ever resolute, attempted to reintroduce dogs to the compound. She started slowly: an Irish cocker spaniel, then two shih-tzus. Each summer she added a few more dogs, hoping to go unnoticed; another cocker, two King Charles spaniels, and a pair of miniature Maltese. Last summer her luck ran out. She brought her two Newfoundlands, Kubla and Buckwheat. Both ran after Grandma and knocked her down. It was us or the dogs. The dogs were banned.

If it had not been for Grandma and Grandpa, we would not have been a family.

Robert and Ethel Kennedy followed closely the path Rose and Joe had taken: they had eleven children together. The youngsters were encouraged to write to their grandmother frequently. Rose appreciated the correspondence and took it as evidence of Ethel's superior mothering skills. She had always felt great empathy for Bobby's wife. According to Rose's former secretary, "Rose felt sorry for Ethel because Ethel had been left with all those children."

Rose's affection for Ethel didn't stop her from trying to influence her daughter-in-law's childrearing practices. She suggested that Ethel feed her offspring in two shifts: an early sitting for the youngest, who merely required feeding, and a later sitting for the older children, Kathleen and Joe, whose needs were more complex. At one point Rose urged Ethel to ban her children from leaving their bicycles outside at night because the damp weather might ruin them.

When rumors began to circulate that Ethel might run for Congress, Rose didn't hide her disapproval. Ethel's place was with her children, not in politics. According to Ethel's biographer, Jerry Oppenheimer, Rose declared, "Ethel has greater responsibility than almost any woman in the world—the moral education of eleven children." She was confident that Ethel's children were being watched over by God and that He in His wisdom would "endow them with a special sense of family responsibility and with an intense desire on the part of the older ones to be examples and guides to the younger ones. [Ethel] will never submit to despair or defeat but will always persevere in her faith, courage, and optimism."

When her grandchildren strayed from the paths prescribed by Rose—and some would stray dramatically—the more distasteful details were kept from her by the family. In the case of David Kennedy and Chris Lawford's drug addictions, Rose was merely told that they had each contracted pneumonia. She chose to believe it. She had always loved David in particular, and being aware of it he once boasted, "Despite the belief in some quarters that Chris Lawford is the favorite grandchild, David Kennedy is in fact Grandma's favorite." He had won Rose's heart, he explained, because he knew the church holidays, was a terrific golfer, and knew exactly where the Pilgrims had landed.

David Kennedy's death from a drug overdose at age 29 is, of all the Kennedy tragedies, one of the most poignant. He was Robert Kennedy's fourth and favorite child, a boy who reminded Bobby a lot of himself. Blond and freckled, the sensitive lad was different from the other nine children Bobby lived to know and love. David was bright, he was good-looking, but in him the Kennedy fighting spirit was tempered by a serene gentleness that Bobby's other kids lacked.

The young boy loved wildflowers and cried easily—never a good idea around Kennedys. His boisterous siblings taunted him and called him a sissy. When Bobby saw David being picked on he would tell him, "Don't let anyone buffalo you. Learn how to fight back and learn how to win." Bobby even took the child for boxing lessons to improve his self-esteem. But although he pushed the boy to toughen up, Bobby hugged his son often. He knew all too well the loneliness that comes from feeling lost in an immense family.

David was the only one of Bobby's children who was not enthusiastic about his father's bid for the presidency. The boy missed Bobby when he toured the country, and his dreams were ridden with images of his father's death. Knowing that David was pining for him, Bobby invited the boy to join him in California for the June 4, 1968 primary. David happily flew to the West Coast. It was on this day that David and Bobby were playing together in the ocean when David was suddenly dragged beneath the water by a fierce current. Bobby, as recounted earlier, rescued his son, who emerged from the scene with a large bump on his head and a feeling of ovewhelming pride in his dad.

The night of June 4, as 12-year-old David sat watching his father's acceptance speech on television, Robert Kennedy was assassinated. The boy sat stunned and alone in the suite at the Ambassador Hotel, watching the horror unfold on the screen before him. There is every reason to believe he never recovered from the trauma.

Ethel reacted to the awful event in standard Kennedy fashion: She buried her feelings and insisted that life go on as usual. That meant David's 13th birthday party on June 15—just days after the murder—would go ahead as planned. The dismal party was a harbinger of the years to come. Ethel refused to talk to David or anyone else about Bobby's death. When her son pressed her about it, she snapped, "It's not a subject I want to discuss." Without Bobby's firm hand to guide the raucous crew of eleven, Ethel slowly lost control over them, especially the wild older boys. She dealt with David by sending him away for the summers—to camp, to Indian reservations, to the lettuce fields of Bobby's friend Cesar Chavez. By the time he was 14, David was smoking marijuana and taking psychedelic drugs. By 18, he was addicted to heroin. He remained in its grip for the rest of his brief life.

A talented writer, David dropped out of Harvard in 1974 and failed to hold onto a job. He bitterly resented what he felt was his scapegoat position in the family and blamed his siblings, many of whom were no strangers to drugs, for not saving him from himself. "When they finally did do something," he complained, "it seemed like it was more to keep me from OD-ing in the street and causing a problem for Teddy's campaign than anything else." The words may sound petulant, but they ring with an authentic, deeply felt pain.

At Easter in 1984 the family gathered in Palm Beach to be with Rose. David, just released from a Minnesota drug rehab program, decided he should make an attempt to join in. Ever the hostess, Rose had a houseful of guests, and 29-year-old David opted to stay in a nearby hotel, the Brazilian Court. It was there his torment finally ended. On April 25, a maid entered his room to find him dead from a lethal combination of drugs.

Rose was not told the circumstances of her grandson's death, and her reaction is not known. At the time she was 94 years old, and her family's main concern was keeping her calm and happy. All Rose's children were by now experts at emotional damage control, and Rose would no doubt have approved of their discretion. After all, it was she who had taught them never to cry in public.

Faith, courage, and optimism, these were the qualities that had seen Rose through tragedies like David's death, and she strived to instill them in each of her grandchildren. Maria Shriver, Eunice and Sargent Shriver's daughter, grew to remember and revere her grandmother's life lessons. When Maria was very young, Rose acted as her personal cheerleader, reminding her that God never sent troubles one couldn't bear. In years to come, Maria often cited her grandmother's sentiments, proudly recalling how much those words had meant to her.

Rose's impact on Maria began when she was only a small child. She had been terrified by her first visit to the dentist and Eunice had told Rose. Rose immediately sent Maria a pep letter, a tour de force of grandmotherly inspiration. She believed in Maria's bravery, Rose wrote, and she reminded the girl of her Uncle Jack's fortitude in the face of excruciating back pain. Rose went on to say how proud she was of the Kennedy teeth and smile, and ended the letter with a dual appeal to Maria's piety (advising her to say a little prayer) and her ability to keep a stiff upper lip. She must be a brave and considerate girl, a help to her mother and an example to her younger brothers. The letter had such a great impact on Maria that she not only memorized the words but framed it and kept it always.

Rose was especially close to Maria in part because she thought she was the most attractive of all her grandchildren. She approved of the young woman's figure (weight was always an issue with Rose), advised her on skin care, and lent her her precious triple-strand pearl necklace, which Maria inherited upon Rose's death.

Rose was one of the first Kennedys to meet Maria's then boyfriend, Arnold Schwarzenegger, in the late 1970s. A champion body builder but not yet a movie star, Schwarzenegger came to Hyannis Port for the weekend. Although polished and self-assured, he was eternally grateful to Rose for her warm welcome and eagerness to put him at his ease.

In an interview with James Delson for *Penthouse* magazine, he later recalled, "Rose Kennedy was great. She speaks perfect German, so we spent the whole weekend talking to each other in my native tongue. We went for several long walks together and talked about Austria at length. The odd thing was that she knew everything about my country. Music, art, opera, even history! I was on my toes every second with her."

Rose may have encouraged her grandchildren to seek suitable mates, but she deplored any lapses in decorum. Any grandchild could incur her wrath if they weren't careful to follow her strict codes of dress and behavior. Once, when Maria dared to lounge around the Hyannis Port compound in a halter dress, a fuming Rose wrote Sargent Shriver demanding an explanation for his daughter's outrageous apparel.

No grandchild was safe from Rose's eagle eye. William Kennedy Smith, long before he became notorious, infuriated his grandmother by drinking Coca Cola—Rose believed the soft drink damaged teeth and issued a decree that none of her children or grandchildren were to drink it. Chris Lawford raised her hackles by requesting breakfast in bed. She was equally peeved when some of the children refused to use plastic glasses by the swimming pool, firing off an irate letter to the offending parties. In the words of her secretary, "Looking back at my notes, it is sad to see how many of Mrs. Kennedy's letters to her grandchildren contained complaints about their behavior or refusal of their requests."

Athletic, determined, and intimidated by neither age nor weather, Rose Kennedy's stamina was legendary among her family. Chris Lawford, the oldest of Patricia Kennedy's children with British actor Peter Lawford, loved walking and playing golf with Rose. He marveled at her energy and her ability to hit the ball in a straight line for around seventy-five yards, then walk rapidly after it. She was in her 80s at the time and Chris only in his late teens, but Rose's energy exhausted him.

"There's no baloney with Grandma," Chris once remarked. "She often reminds me that life is not a bowl of cherries, and that you have to do a lot of things you don't really want to do . . . there are plenty of times when you're going to have to put your head down and just get through it. And she's right. I think her basic philosophy or purpose, in raising her children and now in influencing her grandchildren, has been to try to teach them to teach themselves."

Steve Smith Jr., the oldest son of Jean Kennedy Smith was also awed by his grandmother's physical vitality. In her mid-80s Rose still swam on a regular basis, steeling herself to brave icy, 50-degree water for fifteen minutes a day. Steve Jr. enthused, "It would just freak out all the kids, all these tough little kids throwing footballs and climbing all over the roof and stuff.

They couldn't believe it, but there goes Grandma, 80-something years old, right into the ocean."

Teddy Jr. also had great respect for his grandmother: "I know people who thought of their grandparents as doddering fools who had to be tolerated but were more pathetic than not. It was hard to believe anyone could think that way of a grandparent. It just would never have occurred to us.

"You can tell when my father is around her how important it is to him that she be happy and that she be in touch with us all. It's a major reference point for him. 'Where's Grandma? Let's take Grandma.' She's a fantastic woman and fun to be around when you get her talking about the old days. She has an incredible memory for dates, times, places, and even the most minute details of her surroundings."

Rose's most famous grandchildren were, of course, Caroline Kennedy and John F. Kennedy Jr. Their mother, Jackie, may have been ill at ease with her husband's family (she called his sisters "the rah-rah girls"), but she made sure Rose saw the children as soon as they were born. Just weeks after John Jr.'s birth on November 25, 1960, Jacqueline flew down to Palm Beach with him and Caroline to be with Rose. During their visit they sat for a family portrait by photographer Richard Avedon. Rose later described John as "infinitely adorable," but she worried that the infant might get chilled because his head was exposed for a long time in an unheated living room. Luckily, he emerged unscathed from the photo session.

As John and Caroline grew older, Rose delighted in planning special treats for them. Her pursuit of dignitaries' autographs, which had caused Jack such consternation while in office, was actually done for his children's sake: As a girl she had collected autographs and she believed Caroline and John would grow up to treasure her collection.

After the President's assassination and Jackie's remarriage to Greek shipping tycoon Aristotle Onassis, Rose took great pains to avoid a rift with Jackie. After a time, it became clear that such a problem would not occur—Jackie welcomed her into her life with Ari and encouraged her to stay in touch with John and Caroline.

Consequently, Rose spent several summers on Onassis' private island with Jackie, John, and Caroline. On one trip, John and Caroline had Tim and Maria Shriver as guests and Rose was content to watch them swim, dive, snorkel, and fish. In later years, John Jr. consistently viewed his grandmother through a prism of happy memories. Rose enjoined all her grandchildren to put pen to paper, and when he was 12 John composed a testament to his grandmother. He wrote of how much she had taught him, how much they laughed together, and how much he enjoyed her Boston cream pie. John Jr. especially loved to hear Rose's tales about how bad his father had been when he was a little boy.

Yet despite this promising beginning, Rose's relationship with John paled over the years. According to Barbara Gibson, John's mother "kept John, in particular, away from Rose. . . . Jackie didn't want the children to be too 'Kennedy.' I noticed that she felt most strongly about John not being close to his grandmother. She seemed to want to keep him really close to her. In the end, it worked, because although Caroline and Rose were close—writing to each other regularly—Rose hardly had much to do with John at all."

Rose did, however, witness some of his more high-spirited escapades. When John was only 15, before he had a driver's license, Rose allowed him to drive her and Jackie from the Hyannis Port compound to church. He was stopped by a policeman named Cliggot who demanded to see his license. John airily told him to discuss the matter with a Secret Service agent. Rose's comments are not on record.

During Rose's later years, John made an effort to rekindle their relationship. According to one insider, "Daryl Hannah would spend a lot of time in Hyannis . . . with Rose in her bedroom talking for hours on end. John would pop by several times a day to join in the discussions. Until the very end Rose was a vital part of the family, and everyone wanted her approval."

According to those close to Rose, her feelings for Caroline were exceptionally strong. When she appeared on David Frost's television show, Rose took Caroline with her to observe from the audience. She not only advised Caroline on ethics and religion but also on posture, telling her not to stand with her hands pressed to the side of her body (because that would make her look fat) and to make sure she didn't bite her lower lip and, as a result, get buck teeth.

Jackie had always encouraged Caroline's creative streak, and Rose benefited from it. Caroline continually sent her poems, paintings, and long, detailed letters. When Caroline went to Concord Academy as a boarder, Rose wrote her one of her pep letters, telling her not to be discouraged by the newness of the environment, but to confront the challenge with resolve. Then, recalling her own experiences seventy years before when she, too, had been a Concord student, she told Caroline, "I am sure you will be happy as I was, my dear granddaughter."

Caroline reciprocated her grandmother's warm feelings, and when her first child was born on June 25, 1988, she and her husband, Edwin Schlossberg, named the girl Rose. It was a tragic blow to Caroline when both her beloved mother and her grandmother died within a year of one another. But she finds comfort in honoring both women whenever she can. In 1995, Caroline opened a school in Manhattan dedicated to her mother, and in the future she will surely be called upon to commemorate both mother and grandmother as the occasions arise.

Rose Kennedy never forgot a grandchild's birthday, but as she grew older she often preferred to communicate with them from afar. Their visits ruptured her carefully planned daily routine and interfered with her cherished rituals.

According to Barbara Gibson (who perhaps views Rose with a somewhat jaundiced eye), Rose's feelings about the grandkids ran hot and cold. Gibson recalls one afternoon when Rose was feeling weak and ill and began to question the value of her own life. Gibson countered by mentioning her grandchildren: "After a long pause, she retorted, 'Oh, I don't care about them.' . . . Perhaps the only valid conclusion about Mrs. Kennedy's behavior was that she was in many ways a typical elderly grandmother. She loved her grandchildren, often without understanding them . . . and sometimes without liking them."

No matter how Rose felt about her grandchildren in the deepest recesses of her heart, or how they felt about her, they remained devoted throughout her life. For Rose's 85th birthday in 1975, the grandchildren each contributed to a book of pictures, puzzles, poems, and commentary created especially for her. For her 90th birthday, they staged a parade in Hyannis Port. On another occasion, the children wrote and acted in a play entitled *The Story of Rose*. When Rose turned 100 in 1990, the grandchildren all gathered at her side once again—and the nation celebrated, too. President George Bush declared July 22 Rose Kennedy Day, in honor of the country's most famous grandmother.

17

Celebrating a Century

∽

It was a bright July day in 1990, and a large rose-
and-white tent stood proudly on the grounds of the
Kennedy compound at Hyannis Port. Inside, every ta-
blecloth was printed with roses, while bowls of the lush
flowers graced each table. The 370 family members
and friends gathered inside the softly billowing tent
were in a festive mood: Rose Kennedy was 100 years
old today. Mother, grandmother, great-grandmother,
and founder of modern America's most legendary clan,
she had survived to see a century. This was indeed
cause for celebration, a Sunday to remember.

Earlier in the week a more private celebration had
been held, to which the press were not invited. Bearing
a beautiful bunch of pink roses, Jacqueline Kennedy
Onassis had entered Rose's room, walked straight over

to her, and given her former mother-in-law a big hug. As one observer remembers, "Jackie was radiant. She loved Rose very much and was very respectful toward her."

On this Sunday there would be no Jackie, however, fueling the ever-present rumors of a longtime feud between the two women. Quietly knowing the truth about her earlier visit, Jackie kept out of the limelight.

Yet while there was much to celebrate on this blazing hot July 22—which President Bush had declared Rose Fitzgerald Kennedy Family Appreciation Day—there were also reminders that Rose's life had had more than its share of valleys. Four of her nine children were gone, as was her husband. Her daughter Rosemary was absent for the usual reasons. But although others may have perceived Mrs. Kennedy's life as no bed of roses, publicly she insisted she was content: "I would never change my life for anything—the great rewards more than balance out the difficulties."

Looking around the compound that day, Rose did indeed have much reason to be grateful. Her children, Senator Edward Kennedy, Eunice Shriver, Patricia Lawford, and Jean Smith, had made significant contributions to American life. Rose's wonderful grandchildren, along with twenty-two great-grandchildren, had come to join in the celebration. To hear Maria Shriver tell it, all the attention may have been a bit much for Rose. She had tried to keep out of the spotlight in recent years, and this landmark birthday thrust her right back into it. Shriver said, "I think she's slightly embarrassed, but thrilled because people are making such a fuss over her birthday."

In truth, Rose was conspicuously absent for most of the festivities, making an appearance only briefly, propped in a wheelchair. Her life was now a far cry from what it had been in the glory days. In the mid-1980s Rose had suffered two strokes, the second of which left her semiparalyzed and only dimly aware of the world around her. She spent her time resting in her room, attended by nurses and enjoying daily visits from her priest.

Why, then, a lavish party in her honor? It seemed that her children believed things should go on as normally as possible for Rose, whether or not she could fully appreciate it. And even if she had only a vague comprehension of why the group was gathered there that day, such a celebration was what a woman of her stature deserved, and her family made sure she received it.

Rose's declining health did not dull her family's affection for her. Children and grandchildren alike still looked to Rose—or their memories of her—for inspiration. As Congressman Joseph Kennedy said just before the celebration, "I think she really is the person who holds our family together. She is the person, in all the happy times as well as some of the sad times, that is the glue. She is the one our family has looked to for direction. She is always trying to improve us—if you are going to an interview and your tie is crooked, you can expect to be told. Or when you use the English language in a way that isn't proper, she will be sure to tell you."

If Rose was able to reflect on the assembled guests that day, she surely must have swelled with pride. Granddaughter Maria Shriver was a successful television correspondent, married to an international film star. Caroline Kennedy, too, was happily married and was now president of the Kennedy Library Foundation. Granddaughter Kerry had married Andrew Cuomo, son of the former New York governor. Robert's eldest son, Joseph, was now a Congressman, and his brother, Robert Jr., had dedicated his professional life to helping the environment. Many of the next generation had picked up the torch—they had entered public life and were devoted to helping those less fortunate than they. Joe Kennedy explained at the time that "Grandmother understands that we make contributions as individuals in very different ways and is therefore very willing to encourage each of us in our own way."

There was just one bone of contention Rose had with the younger generation of Kennnedys, and that was their apparent lack of piety. During the last years of her life, according to one close friend, Rose feared her grandchildren did not practice their faith with the same intensity she had. This became obvious when she gave her godson, Charles Van Rensselaer, a special rosary. As Van Rensselaer recalls, "She had just given me a rosary that had once belonged to John Kennedy and urged me to use it often. 'I wish my grandchildren would use the rosaries I have given them,' she said wistfully, 'but they don't.' "

For Senator Edward Kennedy, his mother's 100th birthday was a time to reflect on all the things she had done for him as a mother and for the nation, as a force for liberalism, tolerance, and morality. He chose to share these thoughts with us. Below are some excerpts from that conversation.

SUSAN CRIMP: What are your earliest memories of your mother?

EDWARD KENNEDY: My earliest memories are of my mother reading to me. She always made an effort to spend individual time with each of her children, and it made us feel very special. How she was able to do it with nine of us still amazes me. I remember climbing into her bed and hearing her read stories like *Peter Rabbit*.

S.C.: What values did she teach you?

E.K.: She instilled many values in us and among those were a deep faith in God, a devotion to the family, and a belief that we should always strive to do our best whether we won or lost. She also impressed upon us that we were very fortunate and that we should try and give something back to the country for all it had given us.

S.C.: What is your favorite story about her as you were growing up?

E.K.: I remember a very special idea my mother had to keep stong ties within the family. Obviously, there was quite a difference in ages among my brothers and sisters. My mother was inspired to create a unique relationship between the eldest and the youngest; she asked my older brother Joe to be the godfather to my sister Jean. He was very touched, and when I was born, my brother Jack asked if he could be my godfather. This added an extra dimension to our relationship as brothers.

S.C.: How did your mother hold the family together in times of tragedy?

E.K.: In times of tragedy her faith has been her great strength. It helped the family survive the great grief over the loss of my brothers and sister, and I called on her example to help my son Teddy when he lost his leg to cancer.

My sister Rosemary is mentally retarded, and that was a great sorrow to my mother and to all of us. But she was brought up in our family, and my mother made a great effort to have her included in our activities. If we were going sailing or to a dance, we were encouraged to take her with us for part of the time, and no one spent more time helping her than my mother. Seeing all of her effort made us want to help too.

S.C.: From now on, July 22 has been declared Rose Kennedy Day. What do you hope this will achieve?

E.K.: The Congress of the United States passed a resolution making July 22 Rose Fitzgerald Kennedy Family Appreciation Day. So we hope it will inspire people across the nation to reach out to members of their family and perhaps call them if they are not nearby, have a picnic together, or just pause and reflect about the value of family to us all.

18

Jackie's Farewell

⎰

A year after John Fitzgerald Kennedy's assassination, Jacqueline Kennedy had purchased an opulent apartment on the fourteenth floor of one of Manhattan's most beautiful buildings. She maintained the home for the rest of her life, throughout her marriage to Aristotle Onassis and her years spent as an editor for Doubleday. The dwelling was resplendent with crystal chandeliers, beautiful furnishings, and exquisite works of art. Photographs of Jack, Caroline, and John Jr. were placed lovingly throughout the home, which also featured breathtaking views of Central Park.

The apartment at 1040 Fifth Avenue, for which she had paid $200,000 in 1964, had been the site of many happy moments. Jackie considered it a sanctuary where she invited only her closest friends, and a place in more recent years she shared with her longtime companion, Maurice Templesman. Unquestionably the third most important man in her life, following husbands Jack and Ari, Maurice was as private a person as Jackie. His wealth is estimated to be in the hundreds of millions, his business interests far-reaching. Diamonds are one of his specialties. From Jackie's point of view Maurice was the perfect companion; they shared a love of books, music, long walks, and good conversation. He proved over the years to be a valued friend on whom Jackie counted to shield her from the world. But now, during the bleak November of 1993, Jackie knew that not even Maurice could protect her from the battle to come.

The year had not been a particularly good one; the press, continuing their decades-long obsession with her, had become especially cruel in recent months. In the fall, nephew Ted Kennedy Jr. had gotten married on Block Island. Jackie didn't attend the wedding, and the press howled that she had once again snubbed the Kennedy family.

Although Jackie had long ago steeled herself against these spiteful stories, this one struck an especially hurtful nerve. Far from not wanting to attend young Teddy's wedding, Jackie adored this brave young man who had overcome bone cancer. But recently she had become increasingly tired. Her daily jogs had changed to power walks, and the journey to Block Island threatened to be an exhausting one. She realized, too, what a commotion her arrival would cause. In addition to her son being there with film star Daryl Hannah, Jackie showing up would surely turn Ted Jr.'s special day into a circus. Teddy and his lovely bride, Kiki, deserved their own attention, Jackie felt, and her presence might threaten to eclipse them. So Jackie stayed home, and her absence was interpreted by the media as a snub. Having lived so long in the public eye, she no longer felt the need to explain herself to anyone. Before too long, she knew, the coverage would end.

Jackie had always worked hard to stay healthy, walking constantly, swimming whenever she could, and watching her weight. Given her conscientious lifestyle she had every reason to believe she was physically fit. In 1993, however, something began to feel off. A jog in the park seemed taxing, a horse ride in New Jersey that used to be exhilarating now left her weak and tired. Somehow her body did not move as well, and while she put it down to old age, even Jackie knew there must be a different explanation.

As she had entered middle age Jackie had been plagued by the fear that she would develop the same terrible disease that had struck her mother—Alzheimer's. It never occurred to her that she had anything else to fear, especially at the relatively young age of 64.

At first she thought nothing of the lump in her groin. She was in Virginia visiting friends when she first noticed it, and viewed it as nothing more than a temporary inconvenience. The local doctor prescribed antibiotics, and Jackie promptly put it out of her mind. But the swelling became more severe, and after consulting another doctor Jackie was ordered to check into New York Hospital-Cornell Medical Center. A thorough examination, including a CAT scan, revealed swollen lymph nodes throughout her body. The biopsy that followed told the whole story: She had non-Hodgkin's lymphoma, a deadly form of cancer. The condition was terminal, and Jacqueline knew it. She'd now have to prepare herself, and those she loved, for the worst.

As soon as the diagnosis came in, Jackie thought of Rose. Rose would have known what to do, Rose could have helped her cope with this horror. But Rose was too old now to help her through this, or even to be told about the illness. Her absence made Jackie even more lonely.

Alone in her apartment overlooking the park, Jackie's mind wandered back to Hyannis Port. She thought of Rose Kennedy, a woman who had lived her life in much the same way as Jackie had. Rose had seen Jackie go from debutante to First Lady and had helped her make the journey. She had guided Jackie though her early White House days, and most of all had been there for the fall. Jackie had had no idea how she would survive her husband's death, how she would stay strong for Caroline and John, but Rose was able to advise her. After Bobby's death, Rose proved strong for Jackie again. And it had been Rose who had first given her enthusiastic blessing to Jackie's union with Onassis.

Now, knowing that she might have only a few short months to live, Jackie was determined to go and say farewell to Rose. It was a heart-wrenching journey. Contrary to public opinion, Jackie was a great admirer of Rose, and whenever she could she would make a trip to Hyannis Port to see her.

It must have struck Jackie as ironic that, tower of strength that she was, Rose Kennedy might outlive her. She could not, of course, share this with Rose, nor reveal the true nature of her visit. No one was sure exactly how much Rose was able to comprehend, and there was no point in upsetting her with such sorrowful news. So Jackie traveled to Hyannis Port, a place that brought back so many memories of Jack, to visit Rose for a last good-bye.

Rose wasn't the only person Jackie kept from learning of her cancer. It wasn't until February 10, 1994, that Jackie's spokesperson and friend, Nancy Tuckerman, released a public statement about the illness, but even then she downplayed the situation. "There is every expectation that it [the course of treatment] will be successful," Ms. Tuckerman said. "There is an excellent prognosis. You can never be absolutely sure, but the doctors are very, very optimistic." But as Cindy noted in her *New York Post* column of February 11, 1994, one of Jackie's doctors had called it a "fast-moving" cancer, while another, a cancer specialist, had referred to it as "a very serious case."

What followed were months of hell for Jackie: constant visits to New York Hospital for treatment, all in full view of the world's press, who stalked her every moment of her final year. On May 19, 1994, the end finally arrived. John, Caroline, Teddy, Eunice, Pat, Jean, and other family members all stayed with Jackie and offered their prayers, while thousands of members of the world's media jostled for position on the rainy sidewalks of Fifth Avenue. Teddy had received word on late Wednesday, May 18 that Jackie had taken a turn for the worse and that New York Hospital had told her there was nothing more that they could do. With the same courage and dignity she had demonstrated throughout her life, Jackie made the decision to go home to die. John Kennedy Jr. waited at the doorway for the ambulance that would bring his mother home for the last time. As he did so, Teddy began his journey from Washington, and other family members flew in from across the country. Jackie's priest, Monsignor Bardes, arrived the following morning, and on leaving the apartment he gave the shocking acknowledgment the world had been dreading. "I never wanted this to happen," he told reporters, confirming the assumption that Jackie had indeed been given her last rites. Hundreds of friends came to offer prayers for Jackie: Carly Simon, Rachel (Bunny) Mellon, Palm Beach neighbor Jayne Wrightsman, and virtually every member of the Kennedy clan.

Live satellite trucks lined the entire block between 86th and 85th Streets in order to provide the world with each bit of breaking news. The dismal occasion was made all the more somber by the sight of Caroline and John, who looked devastated. In Washington, President Clinton received hourly updates on Jackie's condition. It seemed that the whole world held a bedside vigil—and everyone was there but Rose.

Together the Kennedys, their friends, and people all over the world prayed for Jackie. At 9:00 P.M. she lapsed into a coma, and at 10:14 the night of May 19, Jacqueline Bouvier Kennedy Onassis was pronounced dead.

All night long strangers gathered outside in the rain, praying, staring, often crying. Upstairs an eerie silence prevailed as Jackie's body was prepared for burial. She was so worried that someone would sneak a photograph that she had insisted on the utmost secrecy for the burial preparations.

The Kennedy family were touched and grateful for the outpouring of emotion over Jackie's passing. Despite his own grief, John Kennedy was outside the front door of his mother's apartment the next morning to thank everyone for their kindness. He read a simple statement: "Last night at around 10:14 my mother passed on. She was surrounded by her friends and her family and her books and the people and things she loved. And she did it her own way and on her own terms, and we all feel lucky that now she's in God's hands."

Meanwhile, hundreds of miles away in Hyannis Port, Rose lay oblivious to what had happened. While the world mourned Jackie's death, her own mother-in-law remained unaware of her passing. Television coverage was dominated by Jackie's final hours, but the plug was pulled from Rose's television set so that she might be spared the news. The next few days were hard ones for the staff in Hyannis Port. Television and family were Rose's main source of entertainment and inspiration these days, and with the television shut off and her family absent, one can only wonder what was going through her mind. If she was cognizant at all she must have recognized the television ploy as one she had first devised years ago to deceive Joe Sr. about Jack's death. But in all likelihood Rose remained innocent of the goings-on.

Over the weekend people lined up outside Jackie's apartment to catch a glimpse of her family in grief. On Monday morning a funeral service was held at St. Ignatius Loyola, the only church near Jackie's home that could accommodate all the people. Following a moving eighty-minute service, Jackie's mahogany casket, adorned with green ferns and a spray of baby's breath, was taken to Arlington National Cemetery where it would lie next to Rose's son, Jack. At graveside John and Caroline knelt, kissed their mother's coffin, and then moved slowly on. John also knelt at his father's grave and touched the black granite stone. He and several family members then walked to Robert's grave. So many of Rose's memories were here, her greatest achievements and reminders of her greatest tragedies. It seemed odd that she was not here too.

The first of many tributes to Jackie was offered by President Clinton. It was simple, sincere, and moving, and summed up many of the qualities that Rose, and all those who knew Jackie, treasured so much in her:

> Jacqueline Kennedy Onassis was a model of courage and dignity for all Americans and all the world. More than any other woman of her time, she captivated our nation and the world with her intelligence, her elegance, and her grace. Even in the face of impossible tragedy, she carried the grief of her family and our entire nation with a calm power that

somehow reassured the rest of us. As First Lady, Mrs. Onassis had an uncommon appreciation of culture that awakened us to all the beauty of our own heritage. She loved art and music, poetry and books, history and architecture, and all matters that enrich the human spirit. She was equally passionate about improving the human condition. She abhorred discrimination of all kinds. And through small, quiet gestures, she stirred a nation's conscience. She was the first First Lady to hire a mentally retarded employee here at the White House. And she made certain for the first time that minority children were all welcome at the White House nursery.

She and President Kennedy embodied such vitality, such optimism, such pride in our nation. They inspired an entire generation of young Americans to see the nobility of helping others and to get involved in public service. We are joined here today at the site of the eternal flame, lit by Jacqueline Kennedy Onassis thirty-one years ago, to bid farewell to this remarkable woman whose life will forever glow in the lives of her fellow Americans. . . .

With admiration, love, and gratitude for the inspirations and dreams she gave to all of us, we say good-bye to Jackie today. May the flame she lit, so long ago, burn brighter here and always brighter in our hearts. God bless you, friend, and farewell.

19

A Rose Still Blooms

∽

"I hear often from people stricken with overwhelming tragedy," Rose once confessed. "When they write, they are frequently close to desolation. I care very deeply about these people. I try to console them as best I can, even though the few words in their broken-hearted letters or in my own replies are able to say so little of what is really in our hearts and minds.

"At times like these, I have always urged others, as I have done myself, to turn to God in faith, knowing that His loving kindness is never far from us and that His providence will protect us against being tested beyond endurance. Faith brings hope, so that we are never really forsaken or alone."

Unbeknownst to most people, Rose Fitzgerald Kennedy spent much of her life trying to help those who had endured pain. Daily, numerous letters would arrive at Rose's home from people who saw in her a source of strength that could somehow save them. She answered each letter, believing that in doing so she was helping to save another soul.

Rose had worked hard to give her children the strength she possessed. Not only was she there for them like the proverbial oak, she endeavored to teach them how to be strong themselves. Her insistence that they not cry in public (not to mention Joe's oft-repeated order that they not cry, period) in many ways seems harsh, but there is no doubt she believed that a thick skin would in the end serve them well—tempered, of course, by an abiding faith in God.

Even Rose could probably not have predicted how much her children would have to endure, and how many times her lessons in endurance would be put to the test. Now, as Rose's days were finally drawing to a close, her remaining children braced themselves for this most profound of losses. No one dreaded the moment more than Teddy.

Senator Kennedy tried to draw on some of the strength Rose had given him as he watched her health deteriorate. Together this mother-and-son team had gone through so much; after Bobby's death twenty-six years earlier, Teddy and Rose had stood at the helm of the family. He had lived through death, disappointments, and scandal, and had weathered most of the storms with unusual grace. Always, Rose had stood behind him, his chief supporter and unflagging fan.

~

An article in the October 1984 *New England Monthly* said of Teddy:

It is admirable, Kennedy's endurance, his lack of self-pity or even of morbidity to which he is so richly entitled. But he cannot be truly serious either, inside this dream, which is so close to a nightmare. He has been too often acted upon, too often the vessel for the desire of others, too seldom alone. The irony is down too deep, and to show seriousness, one must show passion. And he dare not show it lest he be overwhelmed by its consequences.

This was never more true than in October 1994. Teddy's problems were everywhere, but his public persona was as brave as when he had buried his brothers. The most important things in his world were threatened: the life of his mother and his Senate seat. It was terrible timing—and the press was unforgiving. Stories about Senator Kennedy were often cruel and somewhat shortsighted. Teddy had served his community for thirty years, but this year there seemed a real possibility that his opponent, Mitt Romney, might defeat him (Teddy won). Often, according to one person inside the compound, the Senator would talk to his mother about the election. Seated at her bedside he'd share his thoughts with her but was careful never to upset her.

"He'd make her aware of what was going on to a certain extent, but the Senator was most of the time trying to cheer her up," the insider reported. As crucial as the Senate race was, it took a backseat to his concerns for his mother. She was 104, and he knew that it might not be long before he would have to say good-bye.

Looking at his mother tucked up in her hospital bed, in the rose-colored, ocean-facing room, Teddy could not help but reflect on her life. He knew of no one in this century who had lived through so much and affected the course of history through their children as much as she had. It had torn at his heart to see this force of nature cut down by stroke, illness, and age. Her body had betrayed her: The strokes had left her paralyzed on the left side, and she now spent her days upstairs in her room or being taken around in her wheelchair. No one was certain about her mental state. One insider claimed that "she was aware of some things, some things she wasn't. She'd talk to certain people, you could understand her, but her words were slurred. She'd have days when she was good and days when she was bad." Teddy was certain of only one thing: If his independent, strong-willed, often brilliant mother was aware of her condition, she must surely be weary of it.

For the last ten years of her life, Rose required round-the-clock nursing care. She would wake at eleven o'clock, after which her nurses would dress her, then perhaps wheel her outside on the porch or downstairs to the dining area. As all invalids do, she watched a lot of television—her favorite personality being, of course, her granddaughter Maria Shriver. Rose also watched edited videos of past Kennedy triumphs that her family had prepared for her.

Music remained a great source of pleasure, and frequently Rose would be brought downstairs to hear family members play the piano and sing her favorites—"Rosie O' Grady" and "Wild Irish Rose."

The Kennedy clan visited their cherished Rose often; Teddy and Eunice were especially devoted. Every visitor was a blessing, a reminder that the loving care she had lavished on her children and grandchildren was returned by them. It pleased her, too, to reflect that her legacy and the family name would continue long after she was gone.

Over the years Teddy had come to accept calls from the compound concerning his mother's health. Wthin the last decade of her life, there were at least five occasions when everyone expected each day to be her last. Each call that was received at the Senator's office in Washington was treated with the same degree of seriousness, as one Hyannis witness recalls: "We'd call the family and say that she was not doing well and they'd be alerted for this, and all of a sudden, within a day or two, she'd bounce right back. It was kind of amazing." In January 1995, however, there would be no such recovery. When the call arrived at Teddy's office in Washington, he had the feeling that this life-threatening situation would be Rose's last. Monday, January 15, was one of the longest the clan had ever known. Each of Rose's surviving children, with the exception of Rosemary, sat at the bedside praying for their mother. Teddy, Eunice, Pat, and Jean kept up the vigil for six excruciating days, until Sunday, January

22. At 5:30 P.M. Rose died from complications of pneumonia. She was surrounded by Teddy and his wife, Victoria; her daughters, Patricia Kennedy Lawford, Ambassador Jean Kennedy Smith, and Eunice Kennedy Shriver; Robert Kennedy's widow, Ethel; and numerous grandchildren.

There have been many who have misunderstood Rose, and it seems clear that at times Rose did not understand the life that was chosen for her. Yet she lived it, never giving up and finishing the course. In the children and grandchildren who carry within them her compassionate spirit and sense of public duty, she has left every American a precious gift. In her own story, she has left us a timeless source of inspiration.

Notes

Published Texts Consulted:

Cameron, Gail, *Rose: A Biography of Rose Fitzgerald Kennedy*. New York: Putnam, 1971.

David, Lester, *Good Ted, Bad Ted: The Two Faces of Edward M. Kennedy*. Secaucus, NJ: Carol, 1993.

David, Lester, *Jacqueline Kennedy Onassis: A Portrait of Her Private Years*. New York: St. Martin's Press, 1995.

Davis, John H., *The Bouviers: From Waterloo to the Kennedys and Beyond*. Bethesda, MD: National Press Book, 1993.

David, John H., *The Kennedys: Dynasty and Disaster, 1848–1983*. New York: McGraw-Hill, 1984.

Gibson, Barbara, with Caroline Latham, *Life with Rose Kennedy*. New York: Simon and Schuster, 1971.

Kennedy, Rose F., *Times to Remember*. Garden City, NY: Doubleday, 1974.

〜

Latham, Caroline, with Jeannie Sakol, *The Kennedy Encyclopedia*. New York: New American Library, 1989.

Leamer, Lawrence, *The Kennedy Women: The Saga of an American Family*. New York: Villard, 1994.

Leigh, Wendy, *Prince Charming: The John F. Kennedy Jr. Story*. New York: Signet, 1994.

Lorenz, Marita, with Ted Schwarz, *Marita*. New York: Thunder's Mouth Press, 1993.

Schlesinger, Arthur M., *A Thousand Days*. Boston: Houghton Mifflin, 1965.

Weiss, Murray, *Palm Beach Babylon: Sins, Scams and Scandals*. New York: Carol, 1992.

Whalen, Richard J., *The Founding Father: The Story of Joseph P. Kennedy*. New York: New American Library, 1964.

Additional information for this book was obtained through the following sources:

The Boston Globe, The Boston Herald, New York Post, Daily News, The New York Times, Life Magazine, People Magazine, Newsweek, Time Magazine, The Times, The Daily Telegraph, The Independent, The Guardian, The Sunday Telegraph, The Sunday Express, The Daily Express, The Daily Mail, The Mail on Sunday, Hello Magazine, Teale Productions, The British Broadcasting Corporation, and *Paris Match Magazine*.

Index